The Legacy of David Broughton Knox

Edited by Edward Loane

The Latimer Trust

The Legacy of David Broughton Knox © Edward Loane 2018. All rights reserved.

ISBN 978-1-906327-50-7

Cover photo: David Broughton Knox taken by Ramon Williams on the 6th March 1973. Used with permission.

Scripture quotations are from the New International Version, copyright © 2011 and the English Standard Version, copyright © 2001. Used by permission. All rights reserved.

Published by the Latimer Trust May 2018.

The Latimer Trust (formerly Latimer House, Oxford) is a conservative Evangelical research organisation within the Church of England, whose main aim is to promote the history and theology of Anglicanism as understood by those in the Reformed tradition. Interested readers are welcome to consult its website for further details of its many activities.

The Latimer Trust

London N14 4PS UK

Registered Charity: 1084337

Company Number: 4104465

Web: www.latimertrust.org

E-mail: administrator@latimertrust.org

Views expressed in works published by The Latimer Trust are those of the authors and do not necessarily represent the official position of The Latimer Trust.

For the Faculty and Students of Moore College

On 4 December 1857, the aged pioneering missionary, David Livingstone, addressed Cambridge University students for over an hour about his missionary service in Africa. He closed his address with this challenge...

"Do you carry out the work I have begun? I leave it to you."

CONTENTS

Contributors i
Preface v

Legacy 1: Theology

Was Broughton Knox an Amyraldian? Andrew Leslie 1
Ecclesiology: Was Knox Really a Congregationalist? Chase R. Khun 26
Sacramentology: Was Knox Really Anti-Sacraments? Edward Loane 45
An Appreciation of D.B. Knox's "The Everlasting God" Robert Doyle 64
An Awkward Moment: How I Tarnished the Knox Festschrift Peter Jensen 87

Legacy 2: Moore College

Broughton Knox, Theological Education and the Modern Moore College Mark D. Thompson 98

Legacy 3: People - Personal Reflections and Experiences

Paul Barnett 123
Glenn N. Davies 129
Graeme Goldsworthy 135
Graham Cole 139
D. A. Carson 141

Appendices

The Challenge of Writing Broughton Knox's Biography Marcia Cameron 144
Broughton Knox: Some Fragments and Reminiscences Robert Tong 148

Bibliography 158

CONTRIBUTORS

Paul Barnett

Paul Barnett was the Anglican bishop of the North Sydney region and is an eminent New Testament Scholar and Historian. His association with Moore College has extended over more than fifty-five years. He is a graduate of the college, has served on the faculty, and continues to lecture as emeritus faculty.

Marcia Cameron

Marcia Cameron is a Sydney Anglican. She has written local Anglican histories on topics as varied as school, parish and Sydney Diocese. She has also published a biography of D.B. Knox, *An Enigmatic Life: David Broughton Knox, Father of Contemporary Sydney Anglicanism.*

D.A. Carson

D.A. Carson is Research Professor of New Testament at Trinity Evangelical Divinity School in Deerfield, Illinois. He has written and edited numerous books on the Bible and theology. Over the last three decades he has been a regular visitor to Sydney where he has preached and lectured.

Graham A. Cole

Graham A. Cole is Dean and Professor of Biblical and Systematic Theology at Trinity Evangelical School in Deerfield, Illinois. He is a graduate and former faculty member of Moore College. He has also served as Principal of Ridley College, Melbourne and as Anglican Professor of Divinity at Beeson Divinity School.

Glenn N. Davies

Glenn N. Davies is Archbishop of Sydney. He studied at Moore College and served on the faculty for many years where he taught New Testament. He has also ministered in Anglican parishes and as the bishop of North Sydney.

Contributors

Robert Doyle

Robert Doyle is a graduate of Moore College and served on the faculty for several decades. He taught theology and church history. He continues to teach as a visiting lecturer at Moore and George Whitefield College in Cape Town, South Africa.

Graeme Goldsworthy

Graeme Goldsworthy is a graduate of Moore College and served on the faculty for many years. He taught Biblical Theology and has authored a number of influential books in this field. He is now retired and lives in Queensland.

Peter Jensen

Peter Jensen was the Archbishop of Sydney (2001-2013). He is a graduate of Moore College and served on faculty and as Principal prior to becoming Archbishop. He continues his involvement in the college as an emeritus faculty member teaching theology.

Chase R. Kuhn

Chase Kuhn studied at Beeson Divinity School, Alabama before undertaking doctoral studies at Moore College. He joined the faculty of Moore in 2016 teaching theology and Christian ministry. He has recently published *The Ecclesiology of Donald Robinson and D. Broughton Knox*.

Andrew Leslie

Andrew Leslie is a graduate of Moore College and, having completed a PhD at Edinburgh University, joined the faculty of Moore in 2013 where he teaches theology. Prior to his doctoral studies he served in Anglican parishes in Sydney.

Edward Loane

Edward Loane is a graduate of Moore College and, having completed a PhD at Cambridge University, joined the faculty of Moore in 2014 where he teaches theology and church history. He is also an ordained Anglican minister and has served in parish ministry in Sydney and England.

Mark D. Thompson

Mark D. Thompson is the Principal of Moore College. He is a graduate of the college who joined the faculty in 1991 and became Principal in 2013. He has mainly taught theology and for several years has been the head of the college's department of Theology, Philosophy and Ethics.

Robert Tong

Robert Tong is a Sydney Anglican who has served on the governing board of Moore College for several decades. He has been a prominent layman, serving in numerous roles and committees around the diocese. He also works as a solicitor and was a lecturer in law at the University of Technology, Sydney.

PREFACE

26 December 2016 marked the centenary of the birth of David Broughton Knox. He was the eldest son of a clerical family and his father, D.J. Knox, became a prominent evangelical leader in Sydney Diocese. Broughton Knox was a precocious talent and independent thinker who studied Greek and English at Sydney University and then theology at London College of Divinity. In 1947 he joined the faculty of Moore College and his ongoing association with the college was highly significant for the future of the diocese. Marcia Cameron's biography of Knox appropriately employed the subtitle *Father of Contemporary Sydney Anglicanism*. After completing his D.Phil at Oxford, he returned as Moore College vice-principal (1954-1958) and principal (1959-1985), positions from which he influenced generations of clergy. The college also underwent a massive transformation under his leadership and experienced significant growth. In celebration of Knox's contribution, one hundred years after his birth, Moore College Library Day 2016 was devoted to an engagement with 'The Legacy of David Broughton Knox'. The papers from this conference have been edited and compiled in this volume.

The volume is divided into three distinct legacies and includes two appendices. The first legacy is Knox's innovative theological contribution. There are five chapters that engage with Knox's writing. The first four have expanded and refined the research undertaken and delivered at the Library Day. The fifth is similar to the paper delivered on the day itself. The first three chapters seek to engage with, and answer questions relating to, common caricatures of Knox's theology. First, Andrew Leslie deals with the claim that Knox was an Amyraldian. Leslie's expertise in seventeenth century Reformed thought make the complexities of issues surrounding the extent of the atonement easily understandable. He skilfully shows the distinctions between various advocates of hypothetical universalism and identifies Knox's position as being more closely aligned with the English Bishop John Davenant than with Moise Amyraut. Leslie's chapter highlights many of the significant issues that surround this position and he outlines the reasons Knox used to justify holding it.

In chapter two, Chase Kuhn, who has recently published a monograph assessing the ecclesiology of Donald Robinson and Broughton Knox, answers the question of whether Knox was a congregationalist. Kuhn offers an account of Knox's ecclesiology and the exegesis that lies behind it. He highlights Knox's emphasis on the biblical concept of church as a gathering and its eschatological and local manifestations. As such, while congregationalism is a central feature of Knox's ecclesiology, Kuhn argues that Knox was not an advocate for ecclesiastical independence because of his emphasis on Christian fellowship.

In chapter three, I seek to address the question of whether Knox was anti-sacraments. I begin by analysing Knox's writing on sacraments in general, which generally conform to a reformed Anglican position. I then turn to evaluate his thinking about the Lord's Supper and baptism. In both areas he offers a fresh perspective but concludes by endorsing the sacramental practices of the Anglican Church. Knox's most novel position relates to his exegesis of New Testament baptism and I offer an extended critique of his argument on this point.

The Everlasting God was a significant theological work by Broughton Knox and chapter four is dedicated to an extended appraisal of this book by Robert Doyle. Doyle highlights the method employed in the work as well as the significant exegetical positions that are typical of Knox's innovative thinking. Doyle then offers an extended assessment of Knox's argument in relation to contemporary theology.

Peter Jensen has written chapter five and it is included among the theological legacies of Knox, even though it is a personal testimony of Jensen's involvement in Knox's Festschrift, *God Who is Rich in Mercy*. In this chapter, Jensen outlines his desire to include an evaluation of Knox's theology in the Festschrift and how Robert Banks was commissioned to write it. Knox, however, felt that Banks's work did not do his theology justice and wrote a response which has never been published. In Jensen's chapter, he uses the evaluation offered by Banks and the reply written by Knox to explore several points of Knox's theology and clarify a number of issues.

The second of Knox's legacies that this volume explores is his influence on Moore College. Moore was not the only institution that Knox was influential in shaping—he was the founding principal of George Whitefield College in Cape Town and was involved in the establishment of Tyndale House in Cambridge. However, Moore was very much his *Magnum Opus.* When he first began teaching at Moore in 1947 the college was a very small operation with just seventy-two students, a faculty of four and an insubstantial library. Almost forty years later, after Knox's unprecedented twenty-six years as principal, the college had more than doubled its student body, tripled its faculty, established one of the largest theological libraries in the southern hemisphere and purchased a property portfolio more than commensurate with its growth as a residential college for married and single students. This was a remarkable achievement. And yet, as Mark Thompson demonstrates in this chapter, Knox never lost sight of his primary aim in this work—to train gospel ministers to pastor God's people and evangelise the lost. Based on an impressive study of primary sources Thompson clearly shows the development in Knox's program for the college as well as his consistency and devotion to the central task.

The third legacy that is demonstrated in this volume is perhaps the least tangible but the most profound—Knox's impact on people. Throughout his ministry, Knox had an immense impact on a wide variety of people in numerous contexts. The assortment of recollections and tributes gathered here are only a tiny fraction of the testimonial evidence available. Nevertheless, this sample is significant. It shows Knox's impact on internationally renowned churchmen and theologians both in Australia and overseas. Bishop Paul Barnett, Archbishop Glenn Davies, Dr Graeme Goldsworthy, Prof Graham Cole and Prof D.A. Carson each give further insight into Knox's ministry, theological outlook and the legacy that he left.

This volume also includes two appendices. The first is an account by Knox's biographer, Dr Marcia Cameron, of some of the challenges she faced in writing his biography. This is an interesting insight which notes both general issues that would be common to all biographical writing as well as a number of specific issues relating to the subject of her biography. Cameron's chapter is a helpful complement to her biography in highlighting some idiosyncrasies of Broughton Knox and his legacy. The second appendix is provided by Dr Robert Tong who offers the duel perspective of having worked alongside Knox on numerous diocesan committees as well as being a member of Knox's extended family. In this regard, he gives a unique perspective on aspects of Knox's life and family dynamics that expose more of the man's character and convictions.

As stated above, many of these contributions were delivered as papers at the 2016 Moore College Library Day. A number of the papers

vii

have been greatly expanded from what the time restraints of the day could allow. Others have been contributed specifically for this volume and were not presented at the Library Day. One of the many highlights of the day was the display that the Moore College Library exhibited of Knox works and personal papers. Particular thanks must go to the library manager Julie Olston and the college archivist Erin Mollenhauer as well as the other library staff who enriched the day immeasurably. Furthermore, the day marked a significant donation to the library by one of Knox's protégés, the former warden of Tyndale House and internationally renowned scholar Bruce Winter. Knox always encouraged students to read Calvin's *Institutes* and thus it was fitting that on this occasion, Winter made a donation to the library of a rare sixteenth century edition of this classic work.

In concluding this 'Preface', I would just like to relate a personal and (I think) telling discovery that I made while researching my chapter for this volume. D.B. Knox was my grandmother's younger brother and I have known him all my life as Uncle Broughton. Over the course of time various books have been passed down to me by members of the family and as I opened one written by Knox a number of letters and notes fell out which were written by him to other members of the family when he was in his teens and twenties. In one letter he wrote from a voyage and told of his previous twenty-four hours in which he held no less than eight Anglican services. (Nevertheless, he was disappointed because the Roman Catholics 'beat' him by holding thirteen services in the same period.) In another note there is an 'attempt at poetry' written by the teenage Broughton about his second youngest sister, Gloriel. It closes with these lines,

> So we must teach her all we know
> About the Saviour who loves her so
> That when she grows she may be
> Like her aunt, a missionary

I think these two sources highlight both the indefatigable effort that Knox went to for the sake of preaching the gospel as well as his passion for training up other gospel ministers to go out into the world. Gloriel did become a missionary—as did two of Knox's other sisters. The desire young Knox had for his sisters was the same desire he had for countless students that he taught over the years. He taught them all he knew about their saviour who loved them, so that they might tell others.

D.B. Knox (aged 15) with his mother

Edward Loane

Moore College, June 2017

LEGACY 1: THEOLOGY

WAS BROUGHTON KNOX AN AMYRALDIAN?

Andrew Leslie

Introduction

Was Broughton Knox an Amyraldian? It is impossible to be sure. Indeed, Knox did not really know either. When faced with the suggestion that he might be a follower of the famous Frenchman, Moise Amyraut (or Moses Amyraldus), chair of theology at the Academy of Saumur in the 1630s, Knox replied,

> I think it is a little too definite to describe me as a follower of Amyraldus. I have never read anything by Amyraldus; in fact, I don't think there is anything available in English by Amyraldus.[1]

Of course, Knox was wise enough to know that to be labelled an 'Amyraldian' does not necessarily mean you are a disciple of Amyraldus, pointing to one of many terminological difficulties that have plagued the modern evangelical debate concerning the extent of Christ's atonement. In Knox's day, to be called an Amyraldian broadly speaking entailed a commitment to believing Christ's life and death was universal in satisfying the demands of God's justice against sinners, but was only effectually applied to the elect for their salvation alone. The trouble is, as theologians and historians have increasingly come to appreciate, a basic conviction like this can be, and has been, parsed in such a variety of different ways that it is pointless and misleading to associate it with any one figure in particular. Amyraut was neither the father of this theological conviction, nor is his own particular way of expressing it common to every representative of the basic viewpoint. Equally pointless is labelling the alternative to this so-called 'Amyraldianism' 'limited atonement', as if there is just one alternative, or as if every opponent of Amyraldianism would be happy to describe the atonement as something 'limited'—not, at least, without very careful qualification. There are a variety of reasons

---

[1] Typed note to Marcus Loane, D.B. Knox Archive, Samuel Marsden Archives, Moore College, Sydney. Box 16. F. 1.

why these labels have stuck in debates concerning the atonement, but their usefulness is at best limited (excuse the pun!).

I have no intention of resolving this debate here, or even entering it to any great extent. Knox's own statements on the atonement are relatively modest and brief. His best-known and fullest contribution comes from an undated paper delivered at the Tyndale Fellowship of Australia titled, 'Some Aspects of the Atonement'.[2] In it he offers no extensive historical precedent for his view, or any detailed argumentation that might adequately answer or satisfy his critics. For his particular audience, he was simply content to set out his own position along with key supporting arguments in a relatively unfussy and forthright fashion. Indeed, the concise scope of his recorded contribution ought to provide some caution, whether in assessing his position critically, or in citing him as a particular authority on the matter.

Drawing largely from this address to the Tyndale Fellowship, in this essay I intend to outline Knox's key biblical and theological concerns that inform the way he thinks about the atonement. At points it will be useful to highlight some historical connections, although this will be necessarily selective and largely limited to the Early Modern discussion of these issues in the late sixteenth and early seventeenth centuries. Towards the end I will briefly consider the possibility of any connection between Knox's position and the hypothetical universalism of Amyraut. For the bulk of the essay, however, I will argue instead that Knox's position on the atonement bears closer resemblance to a version of 'hypothetical universalism' espoused in England early in the seventeenth century by members of the British delegation to the Synod of Dort, most notably the Anglican Bishop John Davenant (1572-1641). Of course, it is possible that Knox never read anything by Davenant, just as he claimed never to have read anything by Amyraut. That said, Knox certainly did give careful attention to the Canons of Dort, and it is quite likely that his own views were informed by those who themselves were influenced by Davenant and others like him. Even still, Davenant offers a notable point of comparison both because of his connection to the Synod of Dort and to the Church of England, an association he and Knox obviously share in common.

---

[2] D. Broughton Knox, *Selected Works*, ed. Tony Payne and Kirsten Birkett, 2 vols. (Sydney: Matthias Media, 2000/2003). I.253-266.

Knox and the Atonement in Outline

At the outset of his specific discussion of 'limited atonement' in the Tyndale address, Knox is keen to affirm that '[s]ubstitution in sin-bearing' is at the 'centre of the New Testament doctrine of the Atonement.' Underlining this is important as some have argued that any form of universalism as regards the extent of Christ's satisfaction for sin is fundamentally antithetical to a penal substitutionary account of the atonement.[3] Yet whatever may be said about the extent of Christ's satisfaction, Knox remains adamant that the notion of penal substitution is something central to its logic, ruling out all possibility that it somehow remains unfinished or that we might contribute to it in any way.[4] How Knox holds these two things together—a universal satisfaction for sin and penal substitution—will become apparent in due course.

Biblical and Theological Arguments for Universal Satisfaction

Turning to the question at hand, Knox identifies a number of biblical and theological reasons which to his mind require us to regard the atonement as universal in its extent.

Textual Arguments

Leaving precisely what he means by this universality to one side for a moment, Knox alludes to a number of the oft-cited texts which at least point to it in principle. By no means does he offer an ordered or exhaustive list, but he at least hints at or quotes the following within his general argument:

> [...] And the bread that I will give for the life of the world is my flesh. (John 6:51)

> [...] [W]e have concluded this: that one has died for all, therefore all have died; and he died for all, that those who live might no longer live for themselves but for him who for their sake died and was raised. (2 Cor 5:14-15)

---

[3] See, e.g., the essays in: David Gibson and Jonathan Gibson, eds., *From Heaven He Came and Sought Her: Definite Atonement in Historical, Biblical, Theological, and Pastoral Perspective* (Wheaton: Crossway, 2013).
[4] Knox, *Works*, I.260.

> [...] [T]here is one mediator between God and men, the man Christ Jesus, who gave himself as a ransom for all [...]. (1 Tim 2:5-6)
>
> [...] [W]e have our hope set on the living God, who is the Saviour of all people, especially of those who believe. (1 Tim 4:10)
>
> And we have seen and testify that the Father has sent his Son to be the Saviour of the world. (1 John 4:14)[5]

Of the texts usually marshalled to support the universalist case, there are a number of notable omissions from this list (e.g., John 1:29; 3:16; 6:33; Tit 2:11; 1 John 2:1-2). Even still, Knox clearly believes that 'straightforward exegesis' of the verses he mentions, and others like them, will conclude they teach 'the universal extent of the atonement', or that Christ's satisfaction was for every single human being.[6]

By way of aside, it is worth noting that John Calvin, whom Knox cites in support of his own position on the atonement, tends not to read these verses quite this way. As the esteemed historian of Early Modern theology, Richard Muller, has shown, Calvin approaches these texts in a case-by-case fashion, looking at the surrounding context to determine the meaning of their universalising claims.[7] It is not that Calvin would necessarily deny the universal extent of the atonement as a proposition—that is an open question (and one which has been debated extensively); it is simply that in each situation he does not see the texts speaking to this precise issue as 'straightforwardly' as Knox might claim. Indeed, the reality is, within Early Modern Protestantism, as within the subsequent history of Reformed exegesis, these texts have been interpreted in a variety of ways. In fact, Muller believes Heinrich Bullinger and Wolfgang Musculus might offer clearer precedent for the subsequent tradition of exegesis—in which Knox clearly sits—that wishes to read the references to 'all' in texts like 1 Timothy 2:4 and Titus 2:11 as more explicitly embracing every single human being. For instance, where Paul speaks of

---

[5] The two Johannine references are in *The Everlasting God* (ibid., I.110.); the others are in the address 'Some Aspects of the Atonement' (ibid., I.262-263.).
[6] Ibid., I.261.
[7] Richard A. Muller, *Calvin and the Reformed Tradition: On the Work of Christ and the Order of Salvation* (Grand Rapids: Baker Academic, 2012). 70-106.

Christ giving himself as a 'ransom for all' in 1 Timothy 2:6, Bullinger writes that 'this excludes no one except those who exclude themselves by their own ingratitude and faithlessness. Hence, Paul says "he gave himself for all".'[8] Calvin, on the other hand, follows the typically Augustinian pattern of taking this to mean 'all' 'without distinction' (i.e., all 'classes' of people) rather than 'all' 'individuals' without exception.[9]

Another important text for Knox is 2 Peter 2:1, where the apostle makes reference to those false teachers who are destined for destruction, having denied the 'Master who bought them.'[10] The implication is that Christ must have atoned for the sin of those who are clearly reprobate. Once again, by way of historical note, the early Reformed commentaries of Calvin and Bullinger on this verse make no reference to the extent of Christ's satisfaction, suggesting it was neither an obvious point of controversy in the first half of the sixteenth century, nor immediately pertinent to what they regarded as the key message of the verse. Bullinger focuses instead on the way these false teachers specifically deny Christ's saving power, and Calvin considers that their licentious lifestyle denies the very purpose of Christ's redemption.[11] Yet by the time John Owen comes to publish his famous treatise on the atonement a century later, *The Death of Death in the Death of Christ* (1647), the verse certainly had become a

---

[8] Muller mentions Bullinger and Musculus on 1 Tim 2:4 and Tit 2:11 (ibid., 87.), as does Martin Foord, "God wills all people to be saved - or does he? Calvin's reading of 1 Timothy 2:4," in *Engaging with Calvin: Aspects of the Reformer's legacy for today*, ed. Mark D. Thompson (Leicester: Apollos, 2009), 192-195. Bullinger also reads the 'all' (πάντων) in verse 6 the same way, the implication being that he takes 'all' to mean every individual: 'Neminem exclusit hic nisi qui sese excludit sua ingratitudine & perfidia. Hinc Paulis impendit se ait pro omnibus': Heinrich Bullinger, *In D. Apostoli Pauli Ad Thessalonicenses, Timotheum, Titum & Philemonem Epistolas* (Tiguri: Christ. Froschoverus, 1536). I.117.

[9] John Calvin, *Commentaries on the Epistles to Timothy, Titus, and Philemon*, trans. William Pringle (Edinburgh: Calvin Translation Society, 1856). 61-62. Cf., 54-65.

[10] By way of comparison, the editors also add Rom 14:15, 20; 1 Cor 8:11.

[11] Heinrich Bullinger, *In D. Petri Apostoli Epistolam Utramque* (Tiguri: Froschoverum, 1534). 98-100.; John Calvin, *Commentaries on the Catholic Epistles*, trans. John Owen (Edinburgh: Calvin Translation Society, 1855). 393.

disputed text on the extent of Christ's satisfaction, as Owen sets out to refute precisely the kind of inference Knox draws from Peter's statement.[12]

Theological Arguments

In addition to specific texts which to his mind straightforwardly point to the universal extent of Christ's satisfaction, Knox also mounts a number of theological arguments for his case. First, he points to the comprehensive character of the incarnation which has embraced the 'nature which all men share, and not the nature of the elect only.'[13] Secondly, he argues that the completeness or perfection of Christ's obedience to the law means he must have 'fulfilled the obligation which rests on all men equally, and not an obligation which the elect alone have.'[14] Similarly, the comprehensive character of Christ's punishment must fully exhaust the penalty that stands against humanity as a whole and not simply the elect.[15] Finally, in bringing satisfaction for sin, Christ must have fully defeated Satan, thereby destroying his power to hold *any* human being captive to the fear of death, not just his power over the elect (cf., Heb 2:14).[16] In other words, in each of these arguments, Knox implies that any so-called 'limitation' in Christ's satisfaction to the elect would undermine the perfection of his atoning work. Its very perfection demands it be regarded as cosmic and universal in its salvific scope and victory.

This appears to be the way Knox interprets the famous statement traced back to Peter Lombard in the twelfth century, that Christ's atonement was 'sufficient for all'.[17] As a number of scholars have shown, this Lombardian formula had a varied reception within early Reformed discussions on the atonement.[18] At one end of the spectrum, a relative

---

[12] John Owen, *The Works*, ed. William H. Goold (Edinburgh: Johnstone & Hunter, 1850-1855). X.362-364. See also, Francis Turretin, *Institutes of Elenctic Theology*, ed. James T. Dennison Jr., trans. George Musgrave Giger, 3 vols. (Phillipsburg: P&R Publishing, 1992). XIV.xiv.39.

[13] Knox, *Works*, I.260. Cf., 110.

[14] Ibid., I.260. Cf., 109.

[15] Ibid.

[16] Ibid., I.110. Cf., 260.

[17] 'From this [the perfection of Christ's satisfaction] it will be seen that the work of Christ viewed in itself, and apart from its application, is co-extensive with humanity, or, in the old phraseology, "Christ's work is sufficient for all."': ibid., I.260.

[18] Muller actually identifies a taxonomy of seven different positions: Muller,

minority of Reformed thinkers denied it altogether on the grounds that Christ's satisfaction was actually limited to the elect, so that its sufficiency is co-extensive with its efficiency for salvation (e.g., Johann Piscator and Herman Witsius). Others spoke of the atonement possessing a kind of qualified hypothetical or potential sufficiency to satisfy every sin had God wished (on the grounds of its infinite value), even if God only actually intended it to be efficient for the elect (e.g., Calvin, Owen, and to some extent Theodore Beza and Gisbertus Voetius).[19] And at the opposite end of the spectrum there were those like James Ussher, Davenant, and Amyraut who explicitly wished to affirm a real universal sufficiency that means Christ's satisfaction actually makes everyone salvable. Even though Knox approvingly cites William Cunningham's statement about the atonement's inherent sufficiency, being a particularist Cunningham is most certainly only speaking of a hypothetical sufficiency (in fact, Cunningham explicitly resists speculations about the universal value of the atonement apart from its intended application). As for Knox himself,

---

Calvin and the Reformed Tradition, 77 n.22. See also, Michael Lynch, "Early Modern Hypothetical Universalism: Reflections on the *Status Quaestionis* and Modern Scholarship", in *Junius Institute Colloquium* (Calvin Theological Seminary, 2014), 5-8.

[19] On this distinction in Calvin, see most recently, Muller, *Calvin and the Reformed Tradition*, 88-96. Beza did not disapprove of the formula but recognised its inherent ambiguity: see, Raymond A. Blacketer, "Blaming Beza: The Development of Definite Atonement in the Reformed Tradition," in *From Heaven He Came and Sought Her: Definite Atonement in Historical, Biblical, Theological, and Pastoral Perspective*, ed. David Gibson and Jonathan Gibson (Wheaton: Crossway, 2013), 135-136. As Lynch points out, troubled by ambiguity in the Lombardian formula, Voetius aligned himself with Piscator and others who denied any universal sufficiency to the atonement on the grounds that God specifically intended it to be effectual for the elect. Even still, he does grant a kind of hypothetical sufficiency: Lynch, "Hypothetical Universalism" 7. Voetius puts it like this, making it clear that 'sufficiency' is not to be understood as if the satisfaction was actually made for 'each and every person', but in connection to the possibility of it extending to everyone had God wished: 'Sufficientiam aptitudinalem seu potentialem sic intelligendam & explicandam puto, ut non dicatur actu esse obedientia & mors Christi satisfactio, lutrum, meritum, omnibus & singulis praestitum [...]; sed quod potuisset esse sufficiens pro omnibus & singulis, si Deus illud pro iis dare, & Christus pro iis & loco eorum praestare voluisset.': Gisbertus Voetius, *Selectarum disputationum theologicarum*, Five vols. (Utrecht: J. a Waesberge, 1648-67). II.253.

he undoubtedly regards the sufficiency of Christ's death along the universalist lines of Ussher, Davenant, and Amyraut (but this alone does not make him an 'Amyraldian'!).

Furthermore, beyond these inferences Knox draws from the perfection of Christ's atonement, he raises another important theological concern in connection with the Gospel offer. Knox insists that a genuine, universal Gospel offer must entail the claim 'Christ died for you'. Without this 'it would not be possible to extend a universal offer', as a true offer needs to rest on 'adequate grounds, which cannot be less than the death of Christ for those to whom the offer is being made'.[20] More than that, anything less than a universal satisfaction for sin makes it impossible to lay 'on the conscience of the unconverted their duties to repent and believe the gospel', blunting 'the point of evangelism in the pressing home of the claims of Christ.'[21] As he puts it in *The Everlasting God*, to proclaim the possibility of forgiveness must mean there 'is provision of salvation for every hearer of the gospel. For if there were no provision for some, there could be no offer of salvation to these; and if there is no genuine offer, there is no responsibility or blame in rejecting the offer'. If anything, he says, there would only be 'commendation for not being taken in by a spurious invitation to come to Christ for salvation, which in fact is not available.'[22] In other words, for Knox, a genuine offer of salvation to all people must mean every person is potentially salvable, a reality which can only arise from a universal satisfaction for sin.

Universal Satisfaction and the Intention of the Atonement

Having highlighted the biblical and theological reasons Knox identifies as grounds for his broad claim concerning Christ's universal satisfaction, we are now in a position to examine precisely what he means by this claim. To begin with, Knox clearly does not intend to infer from Christ's universal satisfaction that everyone will be saved. Christ's satisfaction does not automatically or effectually result in forgiveness in every case. Certainly, it does not effectually extend to the sin of disbelieving the Gospel. On the other hand, Knox also wants to avoid the Arminian alternative where the atonement only allows for the universal possibility

---

[20] Knox, *Works*, I.261.
[21] Ibid., I.263, 266.
[22] Ibid., I.110.

of salvation without effectually enabling that outcome in any individual case.[23]

How, then, does he navigate between these two extremes? Here Knox introduces the question of divine intention in connection to the atonement. While the atonement brought universal satisfaction for sin, Knox believes God intended it would only be effectually applied to result in forgiveness and salvation for an elect. Against the Arminian universalist, then, Knox readily agrees with the nineteenth century particularist Cunningham, who writes, '[t]he intended destination of the atonement was to effect and secure the forgiveness and salvation of the elect only [...] God did not design or purpose, by sending his Son into the world, to save any but those who are saved.'[24] Indeed, like any particularist, Knox is quite happy to allude to Christ's remark in John's Gospel—'I lay my life down for the sheep' (John 10:15)—referring to the specific intent of his satisfaction to save the elect effectually.[25] Moreover Knox can readily affirm that 'only the elect receive the necessary grace, which grace to repent and believe was merited and purchased by Christ for his sheep; so that ultimately they are the only ones for whom Christ died.'[26] In other words, the objection he has with the so-called 'limited atonement' position is not so much in what it 'states positively'—that Christ's satisfaction was so designed by God to enable and effect repentance and faith in the elect—but in what it 'states negatively'—that Christ's satisfaction was somehow limited to the elect.[27]

In effect, then, as I alluded at the outset, Knox subscribes to a form of Reformed 'hypothetical universalism'. I say 'Reformed' as this kind of approach to the atonement has seldom been explicitly excluded by the classical Reformed confessions, with the notable exception of the *Formula Consensus Helvetica* (1675). From a historical perspective, Knox is certainly right to imply that at least certain kinds of hypothetical universalism can comfortably sit alongside the statements concerning

---

[23] '[...] [T]he Arminian is wrong in what he denies. The Arminian affirms that Christ made all men savable, and denies that he saves any.': ibid., I.261.
[24] William Cunningham, *Works of William Cunningham* (Edinburgh: T&T Clark, 1863). III.364., quoted in Knox, *Works*, I.261-262.
[25] Knox, *Works*, I.262, 263.
[26] Ibid., I.262.
[27] Ibid.

Christ's death in the *Thirty Nine Articles*, the catechism of *The Book of Common Prayer*, and even the Canons of the Synod of Dort. As we shall see further below, notable hypothetical universalists of the early seventeenth century were keen to make precisely that point. Knox himself feels his own position puts him at odds with *The Westminster Confession*,[28] but even with its undeniably particularist accent, recent scholars have rightly shown that its statements do not completely exclude the hypothetical universalist position either. Indeed, this ambiguity may well have been a deliberate concession to those Commissioners who subscribed to precisely that kind of position, like Edmund Calamy and others, who were happy enough to maintain 'their own sense' and endorse it.[29] Finally, although this issue was robustly discussed in the seventeenth century, hypothetical universalists were never treated as having stepped outside the Reformed fellowship. Even Francis Turretin—a figure associated with the staunchly particularist *Formula Consensus Helvetica*—readily adopts a notably more irenic tone towards the hypothetical universalists than his other opponents, referring to them as 'our ministers'.[30] In other words, whatever else may be said about Knox's perspective on the atonement, it needs to be viewed as an authentically Reformed position, if the broad consensus of the sixteenth and seventeenth century confessions is the measure.

Classically, there have been a number of ways hypothetical universalists like Knox have sought to bring together the universal satisfaction of Christ alongside the particularism of its application to the elect. Someone like the Irish Anglican Archbishop of Armagh, James Ussher, maintained that if Christ's satisfaction for sin was universal, his intercession is the specific context in which he limits the application of his satisfaction to bring forgiveness to the elect alone. Knox himself does not seem to make this kind of move.[31] Rather, as we have seen already, he

---

[28] Ibid., I.262-263.

[29] Jonathan D. Moore, "The Extent of the Atonement: English Hypothetical Universalism versus Particular Redemption," in *Drawn into Controversie: Reformed Theological Diversity and Debates Within Seventeenth-Century British Puritanism*, ed. Michael A.G. Haykin and Mark Jones (Göttingen: Vandenhoeck & Ruprecht, 2011), 148-152.

[30] Turretin, *Institutes*, XIV.xiv.6.

[31] On Ussher's theory of the atonement, see, e.g., Jonathan D. Moore, *English Hypothetical Universalism: John Preston and the Softening of Reformed*

prefers to speak of a specific divine 'intention' in relation to Christ's satisfaction that will be effectual for the elect alone, alongside a broader purpose that results in a general and universal satisfaction for sin. Arguably the most distinct historical precedent for this approach to the matter is that of Davenant, Anglican Bishop of Salisbury from 1621-41; a notable champion for a peculiarly English variety of hypothetical universalism.

Knox and Davenant in Comparison

Against Ussher, Davenant maintained that Christ's satisfaction and intercession need to be held together, but in two distinct ways.[32] Here is how he describes these dual intentions in his treatise, *A Dissertation on the Death of Christ*:[33]

> If we consider the whole human race, that is, each and every man, then we say, not only that the death, but the resurrection and intercession of Christ regards them, as to the possibility of their enjoying these benefits, the condition of faith being pre-supposed. If we consider the elect, we affirm that all these things regard them as to the infallibility of enjoying them, because of this condition of faith being destined for, and in time bestowed upon them. Although, therefore, in some special way, the death and resurrection of Christ, with the great treasure of his merits, may be restricted to the elect alone [...], yet it is not to be denied that the death and merits of Christ, who took

---

Theology (Grand Rapids: Eerdmans, 2007). 175-186.; Garry J. Williams, "The Definite Intent of Penal Substitutionary Atonement," in *From Heaven He Came and Sought Her: Definite Atonement in Historical, Biblical, Theological, and Pastoral Perspective*, ed. David Gibson and Jonathan Gibson (Wheaton: Crossway, 2013), 462-464. For a full discussion of Ussher's soteriology, see Richard Snoddy, *The Soteriology of James Ussher: The Act and Object of Saving Faith* (Oxford: Oxford University Press, 2014).

[32] On this point, see Moore, *English Hypothetical*, 193-194.

[33] An English translation of the original Latin version of the treatise, *Dissertatio de Morte Christi* by Josiah Allport is published with his translation of Davenant's *Colossians* commentary: John Davenant, "A Dissertation on the Death of Christ," in *An Exposition of the Epistle of St. Paul to the Colossians* (London: Hamilton, Adams and co., 1831).

the one nature of all, and undertook the one cause of all, are of that kind, that they may be announced, offered, and by faith applied to every individual partaker of human nature.[34]

Like Knox and other hypothetical universalists, Davenant is concerned to bring together his doctrine of the atonement with a conviction that in some very genuine respect, God's redemptive love towards sinners, as it is expressed in the Gospel, is universal and not merely particular. If the Gospel is announceable to all, Davenant insists, it must in some way be applicable to all.[35] Indeed, he makes a point of stressing that the Gospel speaks of Christ being given unconditionally to the whole world as a ransom. The condition 'if you believe' is related to the reception of the gift, not to the giving of the gift itself.[36] On the other hand, like Knox, Davenant is acutely sensitive to the reality that the mere announcement of the Gospel cannot effectually induce faith and repentance, as if the outcome of forgiveness and salvation would somehow rest with some innate power in the human will.[37] For the elect, a further supply of God's grace is required to draw them effectually to faith in the Gospel.

Consequently, as the quotation above suggests, Davenant poses a dual divine intent when it comes to the atonement and Christ's intercession. Not content with the particularist notion of a 'mere' or hypothetical sufficiency, Davenant poses a specific 'ordained' sufficiency to Christ's satisfaction. This ordained sufficiency is necessary, he believes, to make the Gospel offer of salvation a *genuine* offer for all, conditional on belief, rather than an offer that is really only for the elect.[38] Yet the ordained sufficiency of Christ's satisfaction is distinct from a second intention where God wills that the satisfaction of Christ actually be effectual in bringing about repentance, faith, and forgiveness in the elect alone.[39] Notice how he neatly distinguishes between these twin intentions:

> [T]here was in Christ himself a will according to which he willed that his death should regard all men individually; and there was also a will according to which he willed that

---

[34] Ibid., II.373-374.
[35] Ibid., II.380.
[36] Ibid., II.384-5.
[37] Cf., e.g., ibid., II.406-407, 444-405.
[38] Ibid., II.401-404, 408-409.
[39] Ibid., II.380, 396-388.

it should pertain to the elect alone. He willed that it should regard all the posterity of Adam who should be saved, and that it should actually save them all, provided they should embrace it with a true faith. He willed that it should so pertain to the elect alone, that by the merit of it all things which relate to the obtaining of salvation, should be infallibly given to them. And in this sense we confess that the oblation of Christ is of the same extent as the predestination of God.[40]

The resonances between Davenant's and Knox's positions ought to be clear. Both clearly refer to dual divine intentions when it comes to Christ's satisfaction. On the one hand, God intended that the satisfaction would make all individuals actually 'saveable', albeit conditionally—'if they repent and believe', to use Knox's language.[41] On the other, they both refer to a special intent whereby that satisfaction would be effective in procuring the blessings of faith, forgiveness, and actual salvation in the elect. Indeed, returning to an observation above, Knox's conviction that his own position is consistent with the Canons of Dort is supported precisely by the fact that Davenant was part of the British delegation which assiduously fought for a form of words that would be broad enough to allow for these dual intentions in regards to the atonement.[42]

Moreover, in addition to the way Knox and Davenant overlap on the dual divine intentions of Christ's satisfaction, both Davenant and Knox are happy to use the language of 'redemption' in an unqualified sense. [43] Indeed, this is precisely the issue Knox has with *The Westminster*

---

[40] Ibid., II.380.

[41] Knox, *Works*, I.262.

[42] A good deal has been written on Davenant's connection to the Synod of Dort, and the British delegation more broadly: e.g., W. Robert Godfrey, "Tensions within International Calvinism: The Debate on the Atonement at the Synod of Dort, 1618-1619" (Unpublished Ph.D., Stanford University, 1974).; Moore, "Atonement," 144-148.; Lee Gatiss, "The Synod of Dort and Definite Atonement," in *From Heaven He Came and Sought Her: Definite Atonement in Historical, Biblical, Theological, and Pastoral Perspective*, ed. David Gibson and Jonathan Gibson (Wheaton: Crossway, 2013). See too the correspondence published in Anthony Milton, ed. *The British Delegation and the Synod of Dort (1618-19)* (Woodbridge: The Boydell Press, 2005).

[43] E.g., Knox, *Works*, I.110.

Confession, which explicitly restricts this language to the effectual application of Christ's satisfaction in the elect.[44] With the *Confession*, particularists like Owen were especially keen to argue that this restriction is not only theologically coherent but also entirely consistent with scripture.[45] Yet Knox insists it is not only fitting but also necessary to speak of redemption in connection with the universal aspect of Christ's satisfaction.[46] Likewise, Davenant distinguishes between redemption as the payment of the price (which is universal), and the actual deliverance which results when someone believes (which is particular).[47] It is not that either Knox or Davenant fail to recognise an important sense in which redemption language is also uniquely fitting for those to whom it is effectually applied.[48] Indeed, Davenant sharpens this contrast by distinguishing between 'two steps' to 'reconciliation'. Through Christ's universal satisfaction, 'reconciliation is procured for all men', insofar as God is now inclined 'to return into favour' with all people if they believe the Gospel. The second step is when redemption is applied and the condition of faith is fulfilled, bringing a person 'into the paternal favour of God'.[49]

In order to allow for a clear distinction between the universal scope of Christ's satisfaction and its limited application to the elect, Jonathan Moore is right to show that Davenant necessarily wishes to avoid any suggestion that Christ's satisfaction must automatically result in salvation

---

[44] Here is how *The Westminster Confession* puts it: 'As God appointed the elect unto glory, so has He, by the eternal and most free purpose of His will, foreordained all the means thereunto. Wherefore, they who are elected, being fallen in Adam, are redeemed by Christ, are effectually called unto faith in Christ by His Spirit working in due season, are justified, adopted, sanctified, and kept by His power, through faith, unto salvation. Neither are any other redeemed by Christ, effectually called, justified, adopted, sanctified, and saved, but the elect only.' For Knox's objection to this restriction, see ibid., II.262-263.

[45] See, e.g., Owen's extensive discussion in Book III of his *Death of Death* in particular: Owen, *Works*, X.236-293.

[46] Knox, *Works*, I.110, 262, 263, 264.

[47] Davenant, "Dissertatio," II.441. Cf., on the universality of redemption: ibid., II.333, 338-339, 360, 361, 408.

[48] Knox concedes, '[s]alvation and redemption are terms which properly belong to the elect [...].': Knox, *Works*, I.263. Davenant speaks of 'effectual' or 'efficacious' redemption: Davenant, "Dissertatio," II.330, 518, 545, 547-350.

[49] Davenant, "Dissertatio," II.441-442.

for anyone, even the elect. To adapt the title of John Murray's book, for Davenant, redemption accomplished does not *ipso facto* result in redemption applied. This is how Davenant avoids the so-called 'double payment' objection from the particularists: namely, how can God exact punishment on those for whom a ransom has already been paid?[50] For Davenant, the satisfaction of Christ does not *in itself* release anyone from sin and judgment. Rather, God sets up the terms and conditions by which it operates. So, on the one hand, he determines that it makes all people salvable on condition of faith. That means if anyone refuses to believe the Gospel, God is under no obligation to save them.[51] On the other hand, he determines that it will be effectual in saving the elect. Importantly, though, it is not automatically effectual by virtue of the satisfaction itself, but chiefly because of God's will to make it effectual for the elect.[52] In Davenant's mind, to draw an *ipso facto* connection between Christ's satisfaction and its application would mean that everyone must be saved (if the satisfaction were universal), a position he obviously wishes to avoid. Moreover, even if the satisfaction were limited to the elect, Davenant is clearly fearful it would result in a situation where a person is effectively redeemed and justified as soon as the punishment is paid (i.e., before they believe), working against the logic of texts like Ephesians 2:3 which suggest Christians are genuinely 'children of wrath' before they are regenerated and drawn to faith.[53]

---

[50] Davenant does not address this specifically, but it is also the same logic that would answer the objection that if the sin of disbelieving the Gospel is atoned for as part of Christ's universal satisfaction, why is someone damned for disbelief?

[51] So, Davenant, "Dissertatio," II.376. Cf., Moore, *English Hypothetical*, 206-207.

[52] 'But we confess that the death of Christ is infallibly to be applied to the elect alone, because the certainty of the application depends, as to the primary cause, on the secret and eternal act of God in predestinating, and not only on the act of Christ in offering up himself for men.': Davenant, "Dissertatio," II.398. On this point, see Moore, *English Hypothetical*, 195-196.

[53] Notice here, for example, the potential association he sees between an *ipso facto* deliverance and eternal justification: 'Therefore, they are by no means to be attended to who pretend that all men promiscuously are reconciled and placed in a state of grace *by the passion of Christ itself,* or who contend that all the elect, by virtue alone of the same passion, have all their sins pardoned from eternity, since there is no pardon of sins but of those which are committed, nor any pardon of sins committed to be hoped for by any but by those who believe.':

Whilst not so explicit, Knox arguably operates with similar assumptions to Davenant about the nature of Christ's satisfaction. Knox objects to what he calls a 'pecuniary' account of Christ's substitution where it is assumed that payment for sin should automatically result in forgiveness.[54] Elsewhere he insists '[t]he atonement is not quantitative, as though God added up the sins of the elect and placed the penalty for these and these only on Jesus; but the atonement is qualitative. Our Lord experienced fully the penalty for sin.'[55] And like Davenant, he is concerned that from a 'pecuniary' account of substitution, it should 'follow that all the saints are free from the wrath the moment the substitution is made and accepted. Otherwise God would be unjust'[56]—the implication being that forgiveness would be an automatic and immediate consequence of the substitution. Consequently, it is likely that for Knox, a 'qualitative' substitution is such that its effectiveness—both for the elect and the non-elect—ultimately rests with the will or intention of God rather than it being an automatic or necessary consequence of the satisfaction itself.

Arguably Knox (along with other hypothetical universalists) caricatures the particularist account of Christ's satisfaction in alleging it must entail immediate deliverance.[57] Certainly, particularists like Owen have strongly resisted that charge, along with any suggestion of 'eternal

---

Davenant, "Dissertatio," II.453 (emphasis added). As Moore puts it, 'Davenant's concern in all this is to guard against the doctrine of eternal justification that he sees as inherent, if not always actually expressed, in the particular redemptionist system.': Moore, *English Hypothetical*, 194. Cf., Davenant, "Dissertatio," II.447-458; 463-472.

[54] He specifically objects to the way Edwin H. Palmer has framed it along these lines: Knox, *Works*, I.265.

[55] Ibid., I.109.

[56] Ibid., I.265.

[57] Cf., in his critique of Owen's particularism, Neil Chambers presses this objection relentlessly: Neil A. Chambers, "A Critical Examination of John Owen's Argument for Limited Atonement in *The Death of Death in the Death of Christ*" (Unpublished M.Th., Reformed Theological Seminary, 1998), 227-233, 280-221. It is, of course, an old objection famously associated with Faustus Socinus's sixteenth-century critique of penal satisfaction in his *De Jesu Christo Servatore* (published in 1594): cf., Alan W. Gomes, "*De Jesu Christo Servatore*: Faustus Socinus on the Satisfaction of Christ," *Westminster Theological Journal* 55 (1993).

justification'.[58] Moreover, although someone like Owen does hold to a position akin to what Knox calls a 'pecuniary' model, with his insistence that the atonement is an identical punishment (*solutio eiusdem*) and not merely an equivalent punishment (*solutio tantundem*) for sin, even he would recognise that Christ's satisfaction cannot be properly captured in a crassly qualitative and pecuniary fashion, being qualitatively unique in significant respects.[59] Nevertheless, it is true that one of the big issues

---

[58] As Carl Trueman notes, Richard Baxter seized on an unfortunate illustration Owen used in *Death of Death* where he likened the gap between Christ's ransom and person's conversion to the payment of a ransom for a prisoner and the actual delivery of the message to the prisoner some time later. The problem with the illustration is it can make faith appear to be merely an awakening to a reality that already exists, conjuring up fears of so-called 'eternal justification'. In his subsequent correspondence with Baxter, Owen is at pains to clarify—like other particularists—that the covenantal design of the atonement is such that its benefit is not actually received or applied until a person is drawn to faith and united to Christ. In other words, the hypothetical universalist criticism founders at this point by pushing the logic of the commercial metaphor further than a particularist like Owen would be willing to grant. See, Carl R. Trueman, *John Owen: Reformed Catholic, Renaissance Man*, Great Theologians Series (Aldershot: Ashgate, 2007). 116. Cf., 113-118.; also, Carl R. Trueman, "Atonement and the Covenant of Redemption: John Owen on the Nature of Christ's Satisfaction," in *From Heaven He Came and Sought Her: Definite Atonement in Historical, Biblical, Theological, and Pastoral Perspective*, ed. David Gibson and Jonathan Gibson (Wheaton: Crossway, 2013), 208-.; Williams, "Punishment," 511-512. For the original illustration and Baxter's response, see, Owen, *Works*, X.268.; Richard Baxter, *Aphorismes of Justification* (London, 1649). 'Appendix', 155-157. Cf., too, Owen's later clarifications on this matter when responding to Baxter, *Of the Death of Christ.* Owen, *Works*, X.429-479. Related to this, it is also worth noting that while Owen's notion of Christ's 'identical satisfaction' means it liberates a sinner *ipso facto*, he clearly does not understand such *ispo facto* deliverance to be temporally immediate, upon payment, in the fashion Hodge equates with this notion: Charles Hodge, *Systematic Theology* (New York: Charles Scribner and Company, 1872-3). II.470, 576.; cf., Williams, "Punishment," 511 n.584.

[59] Edwin E.M. Tay, *The Priesthood of Christ: Atonement in the Theology of John Owen (1616-1683)* (Milton Keynes: Paternoster, 2014). ins pages. Like Trueman, Tay has the older criticisms of Alan Clifford (and, we might add, Chambers—who is clearly indebted to Clifford) in his sights: cf., Carl R. Trueman, *The Claims of Truth: John Owen's Trinitarian Theology* (Carlisle: Paternoster, 1998). 199-126.; Alan C. Clifford, *Atonement and Justification: English Evangelical*

separating a particularist like Owen and hypothetical universalists like Davenant and Knox, is the precise nature of Christ's satisfaction. If Owen is what we may call a 'realist', drawing an immediate link between the punishment an individual sinner deserves and the substitutionary punishment Christ bears in their place, Knox and Davenant are more 'voluntaristic' in the way they understand this relationship. For them, the substitutionary character of Christ's punishment in place of the sinner's punishment rests chiefly with the will and intention of God to bring the two together rather than with any immediate identity between the two.[60]

In a number of recent pieces advocating a particularist account of the atonement, this appears to be the central contention with hypothetical universalism, and Knox's position in particular. Writers like Steve Jeffery, Mike Ovey, and Andrew Sach, in their book *Pierced for our Transgressions*, and more recently, Garry Williams in the edited volume, *From Heaven He Came and Sought Her*, continue to raise the 'double payment' objection to Knox, because like Owen they assume that a one-to-one, immediate correspondence between an individual sinner's punishment and Christ's substitutionary punishment is basic to the integrity of penal substitutionary atonement. This assumption commits them to a particularist account of Christ's satisfaction: Christ only purchased redemption for those who end up being effectually—even necessarily—redeemed on account of that satisfaction.[61] Yet clearly, Davenant, Knox, and other Reformed hypothetical universalists—who wish to uphold penal substitution—do not see the necessity of such immediate one-to-one correspondence. Historically at least, it is implausible to argue that Owen's *solutio eiusdem* or identical satisfaction approach has been the only acceptable account of penal substitution

---

Theology 1640-1790—An Evaluation (Oxford: Oxford University Press, 1990). 111-121, 125-135, passim.

[60] Although as Trueman observes, even for Owen the effectiveness of the atonement to propitiate sin ultimately rests upon the will and design of God *to make it effective*, yet again mitigating against the charge of a crude commercialism whereby it might somehow 'buy' God's favour: Trueman, *Owen*, 116-117. Cf., Owen, *Works*, X.458.

[61] Steve Jeffrey, Mike Ovey, and Andrew Sach, *Pierced for Our Transgressions: Rediscovering the Glory of Penal Substitution* (Nottingham: IVP, 2007). 276-278.; Williams, "Definite Intent," 480. Cf., 468-471, 480-481.

within the Reformed, or indeed, wider Catholic tradition.[62] Of course, that should not preclude a biblically and theologically informed conversation about what properly constitutes the penal substitutionary character of Christ's satisfaction. Indeed, when the particularist Owen and the hypothetical universalist Richard Baxter locked horns on the atonement, a good deal of their time was taken up debating the precise nature of Christ's satisfaction because they both recognised its significance to the discussion—quite apart from other concerns such as the Gospel offer, and the exegesis of the typical 'proof texts' marshalled for either side in the debate.

This is undoubtedly a conversation which needs to continue. Modern discussions of this issue have not entirely resolved this dilemma between a more realist account of penal substitutionary atonement and the voluntarist alternative. On one side, there are those who assume the realist account is the only viable model without extensively engaging with more voluntarist alternatives in the light of biblical evidence (Williams's recent essays are a notable exception to this trend in their attempt to demonstrate that the typology of sacrifice for sin in Scripture corresponds to specific individuals and sins so that it immediately procures the ransom for the sinner question[63]). On the other hand, the voluntarist too often dismisses the realist position as being excessively 'commercial' or 'pecuniary' without extensive reflection on the theological or biblical concerns behind the metaphor (R.L. Dabney probably offers the last famous attempt to argue seriously for a more voluntarist account of penal satisfaction, although recent writers like Oliver Crisp have attempted to push this discussion forward[64]).

---

[62] In a recent unpublished paper, Michael Lynch raises this objection against the arguments put forward by Williams: Michael J. Lynch, "Not Satisfied: An Analysis and Response to Garry Williams on Penal Substitutionary Atonement and Definite Atonement," (Grand Rapids: Calvin Theological Seminary, 2015). Cf., Williams, "Definite Intent."; Williams, "Punishment.".

[63] Williams, "Definite Intent."; Williams, "Punishment.".

[64] R.L. Dabney, *Syllabus and Notes of the Course of Systematic and Polemic Theology taught in Union Theological Seminary, Virginia* (St. Louis: Presbyterian Publishing Company of St. Louis, 1878). 503-505, 521, 528. Cf., 500-535. Cf., too, Hodge, *Systematic Theology*, II.470-473, 576-477.; more recently, Oliver D. Crisp, *Deviant Calvinism: Broadening Reformed Theology* (Minneapolis: Fortress Press, 2014). 213-233.; or Lynch, "Not Satisfied."

To my knowledge, no one has attempted to construct a hypothetical universalist model which marries a realist stance towards the satisfaction of the elect's sins with a more restricted voluntarist 'application' of that satisfaction to the non-elect. That said, many particularists like Turretin would be happy to say that while Christ's satisfaction specifically answers the sins of the elect, God has intended it underwrite many blessings for the non-elect: due to its infinite worthiness, presumably. 'For it is due to the death of Christ', Turretin writes,

> that the Gospel is preached to every creature, that the gross idolatry of the heathen has been abolished from many parts of the world, that the daring impiety of men is greatly restrained by God's word and that some often obtain many and excellent (though not saving) gifts of the Holy Spirit.[65]

Notice that for someone like Turretin, the limited satisfaction of Christ's death for the elect was nonetheless intended by God to underwrite, amongst other things, the grace of extending the Gospel offer universally. No effectual saving grace is actually communicated in the bare, conditional offer itself. The Gospel offer merely communicates the possibility of being saved, if you believe. It is a real possibility, but only if you believe. A further regenerative work of saving or effectual grace is required to make the possibility a reality, bringing a person to faith—a point with which both Davenant and Knox would surely agree. But rather than underwrite the indiscriminate Gospel offer by universalising Christ's satisfaction so that it also expiates sin indiscriminately, indefinitely, and *in itself* ineffectually—as Knox and Davenant do— Turretin would prefer to maintain that Christ's satisfaction is particular to the elect, while granting that its inherent value enables God to apply it in a more restricted fashion to the non-elect.

So, in summary, perhaps the most central theological issue separating a hypothetical universalist like Knox or Davenant before him concerns the precise character of Christ's satisfaction for sin. Does it pay an equivalent universal price for sin which God may or may not apply as he sees fit (so Knox and Davenant), or does it pay an exact price for the particular sins of the elect which in a sense binds God to save them *on its account?*

---

[65] Turretin, *Institutes*, XIV.xiv.11.

An 'Amyraldian' Knox?

Having highlighted a number of ways in which Knox's position on the atonement aligns with the English hypothetical universalism classically advanced by Davenant, are there any points at which they might differ? In his essay in the volume *From Heaven He Came and Sought Her*, Amar Djaballah arrives at a similar conclusion about Knox as I do: that his position resembles what we have called English hypothetical universalism. But Djaballah also points to one place where Knox sounds more like Amyraut than a classic English hypothetical universalist when remarking that 'the decree of election is logically after the decree of atonement, where also, in fact, it belongs in the working out of the application of salvation.'[66]

Alas, I am unable to provide a detailed outline of Amyraut's own position on the atonement here.[67] He is best known for a speculative construct concerning the divine decrees of redemption. From the various New Testament texts pointing to the universal scope of God's love, Amyraut postulates that God decreed the atonement to propitiate all sin and enable the possibility of salvation to be communicated universally on condition of faith. This may sound similar to what we have seen already in Davenant and Knox, inasmuch as they too refer to a universal divine intention with respect to the atonement. However, Amyraut goes as far as insisting the grace procured by Christ is so exhaustively universal as to enable someone to be saved without the special proclamation of the Gospel. That is to say, Christ's death has made it possible for someone simply to make a sincere response to God's general revelation in nature and be saved, even if they have never heard of Christ. Moreover, Amyraut so stresses the conditionality of this decree—namely, that its effectiveness in bringing actual salvation depends on a person's faithful response—

---

[66] Knox, *Works*, I.265. Cf., 266. See, Amar Djaballah, "Controversy on Universal Grace: A Historical Survey of Moïse Amyraut's *Brief Traitté de la Predestination*," (2013), 198n.156.

[67] For this, the reader could consult Djaballah's essay: Djaballah, "*Brief Traitté*.". Cf., too, Muller, *Calvin and the Reformed Tradition*, 107-160. An older study, which is subject to a number of methodological criticisms, is Brian G. Armstrong, *Calvinism and the Amyraut Heresy: Protestant Scholasticism and Humanism in Seventeenth-century France* (Madison: University of Wisconsin Press, 1969).

that he readily admits it may be 'frustrated' when people refuse to believe. Indeed, that is precisely what happens on a universal scale, due to human depravity. Amyraut writes, '[t]he nature of humanity was such that if God, in sending his Son into the world, had only determined to offer him as Redeemer equally and universally to all [...] the sufferings of his Son would have been entirely in vain'.[68] Foreseeing this outcome, God then makes a second decree to provide the grace necessary to fulfil the condition of faith in an elect so the atonement might be applied to them effectually.

While Amyraut's position on the atonement did not result in any formal exclusion from the Reformed fellowship, it did face considerable criticism. In a very important respect, he distances himself from the Arminian position by insisting on a universal inability to respond favourably to God's atoning grace. But as his detractors were quick to point out, he closely echoes the Arminian view insofar as the effectiveness of Christ's atonement entirely hinges on the human response of faith, even if that faith happens to be enabled by God's grace. Even more alarming to his Reformed audience was the speculation that someone could hypothetically be saved without conscious faith in Christ. Indeed, as Muller notes, Amyraut's chief opponent, Pierre du Moulin quipped that if Arminius is 'Semi-Pelagian in all things', Amyraut is at least 'three quarters' Semi-Pelagian![69]

Amyraut's position also faced a number of other serious and related objections.[70] His opponents objected to the prospect that God's universal will to save all through the work of Christ might actually be defeated by human obstinacy, only to be retrieved by a subsequent decree of election. Not only does this threaten God's immutable sovereignty, they felt, it also causes an inevitable tension between the incarnate Son's universal, but ultimately ineffectual mediatorial work, versus the particularist work of the Father and the Spirit to fulfil the condition of faith in an elect. As Christ goes to the cross in fulfilment of a purely indefinite decree, he is effectively agnostic about those to whom his work will eventually apply. Not only that, his inability to procure the gift of faith

---

[68] From his *Brief Traitté de la Predestination et de ses principales dependances*, chapter 9, quoted in Djaballah, "*Brief Traitté*," 184.
[69] Muller, *Calvin and the Reformed Tradition*, 155.
[70] For these kinds of objections and others, see, e.g., Turretin, *Institutes*, XIV.xiv.9-54.

means the Son's mediatorial office is essentially deprived of the divine power necessary for his ultimate union to the elect. God is forced to work outside the mediatorial office of Christ to make his work effectual in the elect. Indeed, strictly speaking it would no longer be possible to say with Paul that Christians are chosen *in Christ* 'before the creation of the world to be holy and blameless in his sight' (Eph 1:4).

Returning to Knox, is there any sense in which his statement about the order of decrees resembles that of Amyraut? To my mind, it would certainly be possible to put an Amyraldian gloss on his prioritising of the decree of a universal atonement over the decree of election. But there are several reasons why I believe this would be uncharitable. Foremost of these is Knox's explicit statement that Christ came with the specific intent of saving 'his people from their sins'.[71] Indeed, for Knox this intention of Christ was fully effectual. Like Davenant and the Synod of Dort, he insists the 'grace to repent and believe was merited and purchased by Christ' specifically 'for his sheep'.[72] Amyraut would be unable to say that. In fact, Davenant himself foresaw the objection that the purely indefinite work of Christ might abstract him from any particular divine will to make it applicable to the elect. It was very important to Davenant that Christ fully participates in the dual divine intentions for his satisfaction, both to ensure his satisfaction is fully effectual in procuring salvation for the elect, and to safeguard against any division of the Son's mediatorial work from the Father and the Spirit's application of that work to the elect.[73] Nevertheless, Davenant was still quite happy to suggest a structural precedence in the divine will, placing the general universal intention for the atonement to make all people salvable on condition of faith, before the specific intention to ensure it would effectually save the elect.[74] Knox is certainly not so explicit as

---

[71] Knox, *Works*, I.262.

[72] Ibid. In his critique of Owen, Chambers objects to the notion that Christ's death purchased or procured the gift of faith. In this respect, the hypothetical universalism of Davenant and Knox aligns with the position of Owen and Dort, whilst Chambers moves in a more Amyraldian direction on this matter: Chambers, "Critical Examination," 190-234.

[73] Note, e.g., Davenant, "Dissertatio," II.398, 518-399, 530, 556-397. Cf., Moore, *English Hypothetical*, 193, 197, 201.

[74] E.g., Davenant, "Dissertatio," II.363-364, 555-366. Cf., Moore, *English Hypothetical*, 205-206.

Davenant in stating or even, perhaps, anticipating these issues. And it is true that some of his statements, such as 'the atonement is general, its application particular',[75] are insufficiently precise to rule out an Amyraldian gloss. Yet, his willingness to speak of Christ's specific intention to die effectually for the elect brings a clarity that unambiguously aligns his position with the hypothetical universalism of Davenant rather than Amyraut.

Conclusion

In outlining his views on the atonement, Knox identifies several biblical and theological principles he is keen to preserve. On the one hand, there are a number of New Testament texts which to his mind straightforwardly suggest that Christ's satisfaction for sin was universal and indiscriminate in its scope. On the other hand, he feels a similar theological inference must be drawn from the comprehensive character of Christ's person and redemptive work on behalf of all humanity. Moreover, the universality of Christ's satisfaction is essential to underwrite both the authenticity of the indiscriminate Gospel call and the accountability that attends every human response to that call. Since a purely particular satisfaction cuts against the grain of all these principles, in his view it must be set aside.

Even still, for Knox the indiscriminate, universal benefit of Christ's satisfaction goes no further than underwriting the Gospel call. It does not entail the prospect of universal salvation since God only ever intended it be applied effectually to his elect. In that sense, Knox's position may be styled as a version of Reformed 'hypothetical universalism'. Yet, in contrast to an older perception that all forms of hypothetical universalism - Knox's included - equate to 'Amyraldianism', I have attempted to show that a more proximate historical precedent for Knox's view is a peculiarly English cast of hypothetical universalism classically proposed by Bishop Davenant and the British delegation at the Synod of Dort. For Davenant, as for Knox, God's intent for Christ's satisfaction was both universal in one respect and particular in another.

---

[75] Knox, *Works*, I.265. Similarly, his comment to Marcus Loane suffers on this score: 'I believe the atonement covers all of humanity, not merely the elect of God. But it is applied by God only to those whom He has chosen, i.e. the limitation is not in the work of Christ but in the application of the work of Christ'. A strict Amyraldian could agree with this. To preclude the Amyraldian reading, Knox would need to add that the application of Christ's work was always an intended result of his work, and that Christ himself fully shared in this intention.

As a universal, indiscriminate ransom for sin, it was intended to provide the genuine possibility of salvation for every individual, if they believe the Gospel. At the same time, even though it bought redemption for all sin, God also intended that it should only apply effectually to his elect. This is notably different from Amyraut's more idiosyncratic (and controversial) version of hypothetical universalism in its refusal to speculate about universal grace, or a sequence of decrees, beginning with one of conditional redemption which then needs to be salvaged by a further decree of election to faith.

As we have seen, aside from the exegesis of various texts—concerning which interpreters have leaned in different directions—one of the key issues separating the hypothetical universalism of Davenant and Knox from the particularism of other Reformed thinkers like Owen is the precise nature of Christ's penal satisfaction. For the hypothetical universalist, Christ's satisfaction cannot *in itself* guarantee the salvation of anyone. Its effectiveness to bring forgiveness and salvation rests purely with the will and intention of God to apply it that way rather than in any necessary connection between the two. On the other hand, the particularist will insist that however infinitely valuable it may be, Christ's satisfaction was specifically designed to answer the sin of the elect, necessarily resulting in their ransom. Leaving aside the volley of easy pejoratives that have typically ricocheted between the participants in this debate—accusations of proof texting, 'double payment' for sin, crass 'pecuniary' commercialism and the like—this is arguably the central question that needs to be resolved through careful biblical and theological argumentation. Knox's statements on the atonement are all too brief to resolve this issue satisfactorily. Having assumed that a purely 'qualitative' and indefinite atonement makes best sense of the biblical and theological principles he wishes to uphold, he is not especially concerned to anticipate or respond to any objections that might legitimately arise.

Ecclesiology: Was Knox Really a Congregationalist?

Chase R. Kuhn

Introduction

Was Broughton Knox a congregationalist? Yes. The short answer is that he was a congregationalist in a very strict sense. However, what this means for his ecclesiology is different to what has been the critique and accusation of many. This chapter will explore some of the core tenets of Knox's ecclesiology that demonstrate his congregationalism. Clarity will emerge regarding what was *not* implicit in his ecclesiology. It will be argued that Knox's position was congregational, but not parochial.[76]

Various hypotheses have been put forward about the genesis of Knox's ecclesiology, most notably by Bill Lawton.[77] In the 1980s, he proposed that Broughton Knox, through his father D.J. Knox, was the theological progeny of Nathaniel Jones. Lawton claimed that Jones's theology was indebted to his early spiritual roots in the UK, and ongoing associations with the Plymouth Brethren at the Katoomba Convention.[78] It was a 'little flock theology' that continued 'to disturb Sydney Anglicanism' throughout the twentieth century through Jones's successors, namely the Knox and Robinson family lines.[79] Elsewhere, I have demonstrated that, while Lawton's work is a useful introduction to the Anglicanism in Sydney at the turn of the twentieth century, he has

---

[76] This chapter is in large part an adaption of previous research published in Chase R. Kuhn, *The Ecclesiology of Donald Robinson and D. Broughton Knox: Exposition, Analysis and Theological Evaluation* (Eugene: Wipf & Stock, 2017). Used by permission of Wipf and Stock Publishers. www.wipfandstock.com.

[77] It should be noted that Lawton's work is responsible for many of the depictions of Knox's ecclesiology that would follow, including that of Muriel Porter. Muriel Porter, *Sydney Anglicans and the Threat to World Anglicanism* (Farnham, Surrey: Ashgate, 2011). 40.

[78] William Lawton, *The Better Time to Be: Utopian Attitudes to Society Among Sydney Anglicans 1885-1914* (Kensington, NSW: UNSW Press, 1990). 72.

[79] William Lawton, "Nathaniel Jones," in *God Who is Rich in Mercy: Essays Presented to Dr. D.B. Knox*, ed. Peter T. O'Brien and David G. Peterson (Hombush, N.S.W.: Lancer Books, 1986), 364.

misrepresented Jones as well as his successors.[80] None of his claims are supported by primary source evidence, nor are they supported by testimony.[81]

Biblical Theological Foundation

Knox's ecclesiology was formulated, not from a Brethren inheritance, but rather from his own biblical theological method. This formulation was in conversation with his friend and colleague Donald Robinson.[82] From analysis of both scholar's works, it appears that Robinson did the heavy lifting of biblical theology, while Knox worked to develop and expound the theological implications of that foundation. At the core, was an understanding that the church is a gathering. Nothing more, nothing less. This was determined linguistically, studying the usage of *ekklēsia* across the canon, both in the LXX and New Testament with attention also given to the Hebrew correlates.[83] Robinson and Knox recognized that *ekklēsia*, a gathering of people, had a special function in the plans and purposes of God; in his redemptive work, God gathers a people unto Himself— Indeed, *before* Himself. Knox identified Matthew 16:18 as the most important (and most controversial!) ecclesiological text in the Bible.[84]

In the Old Testament the constitutive event of the church was the Lord covenanting with his people at Mt. Sinai. In that episode, the Lord asked Moses to *gather* the people before him on the mountain. Deuteronomy 4:10 referred to this as the 'day of the church.'[85] Knox believed that this gathering before Mount Sinai, the 'mountainous rock,' was the prototype for the gathering that Christ was establishing.[86] Knox saw a direct

---

[80] Kuhn, *Ecclesiology of Robinson and Knox*, Chapter 1.

[81] Marcus Loane, "Review of William Lawton's *Better Time to Be*," *Lucas: An Evangelical History Review* no. 11 (Feb 1991): 42.

[82] The ecclesiology of Knox has often been coupled with Robinson's and given the colloquial name the "Knox-Robinson Ecclesiology."

[83] For a detailed analysis see Kuhn, *Ecclesiology of Robinson and Knox*, 52–56, 98–105.

[84] D. Broughton Knox, "The Church, the Churches and the Denominations of the Churches," *Reformed Theological Review* 48(1989): 15–25. in Knox, *Works*, II.85. (page citations are to the reprint edition).

[85] This is the title ascribed to the event in the LXX, which is not contained in the BHS.

[86] Knox, *Works*, II.85–88.

correlation of the language used by Jesus in Matthew 16 with the language of 'the day of the church.' He believed that this extended beyond simple similarities of vocabulary, of which 'rock' and 'church' are prominent. But the grammar of Matthew 16 also serves as an indication that the Sinai gathering is in view. What normally reads in English Bibles, 'on this Rock I will build my church,' Knox understood as '*before* this Rock I will build my church.'[87] The church, or gathering, Christ is establishing is before himself. Christ's presence with his people is essential to the constitution of the church, as it is his presence that demarcates the church from any other gathering.

Moving from this analysis of Matthew 16, Knox examined how his conclusions were developed later in the New Testament. If the Old Testament type of *ekklēsia* at Sinai is fulfilled in what Christ is building himself, what does this mean for Christians? Knox found the answer in Hebrews 12.[88]

> For you have not come to what may be touched ... You have come[89] to mount Zion and to the city of the living God, the heavenly Jerusalem, and to innumerable angels in festal gathering, and to the assembly [church] of the firstborn who are enrolled in heaven, and to God, the judge of all, and to the spirits of the righteous made perfect, and to Jesus, the mediator of a new covenant, and to the sprinkled blood that speaks a better word than the blood of Abel. (Heb. 12:18a, 22-24 ESV).

---

[87] D. Broughton Knox, "De-Mythologizing the Church," *Reformed Theological Review* 32(1973): 48–55. Reprint in Knox, *Works*, II.25. (page citations are to the reprint edition).
See my engagement with the viability of this rendering of *epi* in Kuhn, *Ecclesiology of Robinson and Knox*, 185f.

[88] D. Broughton Knox, *The Thirty-Nine Articles*, 2nd ed. (Sydney: Anglican Information Office, 1976). Reprint in Knox, *Works*, II.141. (page citations are to the reprint edition).

[89] 'You have come' is the second person plural perfect indicative form of the verb *proserchomai*. This perfect form connotes a completed action with present consequence. For further discussion, see Kuhn, *Ecclesiology of Robinson and Knox*, 188–189.

The church in Hebrews is contrasted with the OT gathering at Sinai. The fundamental shift is one from a physical reality in the Old Testament church, to a spiritual reality in the New Testament church. Knox believed that according to Hebrews 12 the earthly church has an immediate correlation with the heavenly church.[90]

The Primacy of the Heavenly Gathering

It is the importance of the presence of Christ that made the heavenly church so prominent in Knox's ecclesiology. Knox believed that if God is gathering people before Christ, then the church is to be conceived of primarily as a heavenly reality, as this is where Christ is currently. Biblically, Knox recognized this reality in Ephesians 2:5-6 (amongst other texts, cf. Heb. 12:18-24; Col. 3:1-4), which declares that God has 'made us alive together with Christ—by grace you have been saved—and raised us up with him and seated us with him in the heavenly places in Christ Jesus' (ESV). Further to biblical evidence, Knox believed that it is the heavenly church that is confessed in the Nicene Creed. '"I believe one catholick and apostolick church." Its principle of unity is the fact that Christ has assembled it around himself. It is logically impossible for him to assemble two churches; for Christ is to be primarily thought of as in one place only, that is, in heaven, if we are to use biblical imagery, which is the only imagery available in a matter which transcends experience.'[91] Therefore, the perfection (fullness) of the church is known in heaven.[92] But this does not mean that the earthly church is false or any less real. The heavenly church finds full expression in the earthly gatherings of local churches. The constitutive element remains: Christ promises to be present where two or more are gathered (Matt. 18:20). Therefore, the church on earth is the occasion when believers meet around the Word of Christ in the presence of Christ, giving expression to the heavenly church.

The Local Church – Expression of the Heavenly

Knox wrote assertively of the fullness of the local church. In other words, the local church is not in any way deficient; it is the full expression of *the*

---

[90] Knox, *Works*, II.26.

[91] Ibid., II.142.

[92] Knox also commented on the Apostles' Creed, identifying the heavenly church with the 'holy catholic church,' and the 'communion of saints' with the earthly congregations. See ibid.

church.[93] The local church reflects the heavenly gathering and is promised the presence of Christ, which is *the* defining element of the church (Matt. 18:20). Knox's concern in expressing this truth was to establish that there is no ecclesial reality to be sought on earth *beyond* the local church (e.g. institutional). Christ is present wherever two or three are gathered. These gatherings are *the* church. There is no set number that equates to the fullness of ecclesial expression (e.g. every believer on earth). This is not to say that the experience of God in the local church is perfect. Knox wrote, 'Yet though our fellowship with God is true and precious, it is not yet full. We see only as it were in a dull mirror, and we look forward to seeing face to face (1 Cor 13:12), to seeing Jesus as he is (1 John 3:2), of knowing as fully as he knows us (1 Cor 13:12).'[94] There is a goal towards which the local church is heading; fellowship with the Triune God will not be enjoyed in the fullest sense until the eschaton. But if the church is the fullness of the heavenly church, how is it that the fullness of the heavenly is not experienced in the earthly? Does not the anticipation of fullness of the heavenly express a lack in the earthly?

Following his identification of the creedal properties with the heavenly church, the heavenly church is the only church capable of realizing the perfections confessed. This is not a diminished reality in the earthly church, but an actualization appropriate to its dimension. For instance, unity is expressed in a manner appropriate for the earthly dimension: in the local congregation. Fuller unity of believers in a *universal* sense is only possible in the place where all are actually congregated: in the heavenly church. Thus, as the creed is declared in faith, many of the ecclesial properties confessed remain objects of faith until the Parousia when they will turn from faith to sight.

Knox was concerned that modern idiom ascribed more to the church than was indicated by the New Testament. The popular notion of the church was something universal that existed on earth. Knox argued that this notion was inconceivable as a universal (global) church could not

---

[93] D. Broughton Knox, "The Biblical Concept of Fellowship," in *Explorations 2: Church, Worship, and the Local Congregation*, ed. B.G. Webb (Sydney: Lancer, 1987), 59–82. reprinted in Knox, *Works*, II.82. (page citations are to the reprint edition).
[94] Ibid., II.82.

and would not ever gather, and gathering is *the* definitive activity of the church.

Developing his thought in contrast to the inaccurate idiom of his day, Knox explained that the church must be understood with regards to time and space. The church is something that happens *in* time. It is constant in the heavenly realms as believers are presently seated, spiritually, in the heavenly places where Christ is (Eph. 2:6). On earth, the church happens intermittently. It gathers regularly, giving expression to the heavenly gathering, but it does not remain assembled. This distinction of time in Knox's thought can generate potential confusion. One activity is constant and one is intermittent, yet both are speaking of the same ultimate reality, and both are experienced by the believer. How is this so? How can one (the heavenly) occasionally find expression in the other (the earthly), and yet continue without expression when the other disbands? It is likely that Knox understood the heavenly and spiritual reality of believers to be a positional experience of Christians on earth. When these Christians gather they give expression to the standing that they have *spiritually* in Christ.

Likewise, both gatherings happen in space. They require presence, though this presence is not necessarily physical by both parties. The heavenly gathering is presently a spiritual reality, with all believers present in the Spirit before Christ where he is seated physically. This spiritual presence is often referred to in Scripture as believers' status of being 'in Christ.' On earth, believers gather physically to give expression to their spiritual presence before Christ in heaven. In the midst of that physical gathering, Christ promises his spiritual presence. Like time, Knox's understanding of space may initially cause some confusion. How is it that there is 'presence' spiritually if spiritual implies immaterial? Does not space require matter? Again, the explanation of Knox's thought requires the recognition of the positional reality that believers have 'in Christ' in the heavenly places, where he is physically. Knox understood there to be a reciprocal relationship in which believers are present spiritually in the heavenly places where Christ is present physically, and believers are present physically in the earthly gatherings where Christ is present spiritually.[95]

---

[95] D. Broughton Knox, "The Church," Protestant Faith Radio Broadcast 22 March 1970, published in ibid., II.19–20.

It is the Holy Spirit who draws believers together into a congregation. Thus, the local church gives demonstration in time and space of the work that God is doing eternally.

> Being in Christ's presence, through his Spirit present in them, naturally draws Christians into each other's company. They meet together in his name, and Christ is there in each. Thus the local church forms spontaneously as an expression, in the sphere of time and space, of the eternal reality of fellowship with God which each has, and who is in each. Christians are never exhorted in the New Testament to become members of the church, for that is synonymous with being Christ's. But they are exhorted to give expression to their membership by being present in the local church, or gathering, of Christ round himself.[96]

Knox believed that the local gathering was imperative for believers for both obedience (Heb. 10:25), and for fellowship with Christ in the company of others (Matt. 18:20). This imperative for Christians to gather is an identification of the primacy of the heavenly church; Christians don't need to be told to join the church—they know they belong—but they do need to be told to give expression to that reality.

Knox's ecclesiology has been severely criticized because of his emphasis on the church as primarily a heavenly reality. Kevin Giles has been the most forthright with his criticism. Giles believes that Knox's focus on the heavenly church, in texts like Hebrews 12:18-24, unnecessarily restricted the church on earth to a local only reality.[97] Giles's ultimate critique of Knox is that his ecclesiology was platonic, with an overemphasis on the duality of realms.[98] He argues that the notion of a heavenly church in the New Testament remains an eschatological reality; not something experienced, but rather anticipated, in time by believers. Knox, however, was not content with such an explanation, understanding Hebrews 12 to be an actual experience of the believers in time, for Christ is building his church where he is, and he is in heaven. The experience of this reality, for Knox, was something that occurs

---

[96] Ibid., II.89.
[97] Kevin Giles, *What on Earth is the Church?: An Exploration in New Testament Theology* (Eugene: Wipf & Stock, 1995). 156.
[98] See ibid., 14, 190–195.

spiritually. If believers are present with Christ, and Christ is present with them, then the only explanation is that this presence occurs in the Spirit. The ontological connection of the heavenly and the earthly is the presence of Christ, and this is mediated by the Spirit.

Catholicity

What is to be said of Knox's position regarding the universal global church, and even more specifically to Giles's accusations of Platonism? Knox did not believe in a universal church on earth; Giles was accurate in his critique. However, the foundation of Giles's critique is what remains to be questioned. Regarding the platonic nature of Knox's ecclesiology, Knox did not believe that the heavenly was the perfect form of the earthly. In fact, the one (earthly) is a legitimate expression of the other (heavenly). This is because central to Knox's ecclesiology was the understanding that the church is the gathering of God's people where Christ is. Christ is *really* present with believers on earth even after his ascension, *by* his Holy Spirit. Likewise, Christians *are* currently in the heavenly places with Christ *by* his Spirit, enjoying the benefits of his heavenly session even as they live on earth. There is, of course, a future realization of these two realities, better known as the consummation, which will come when Christ is wed to his bride. But the bride does not change, nor the bridegroom. And the union between them, even when present physically with one another, will always be spiritual – that is, by the Holy Spirit.

To properly understand Knox's congregationalism—and avoid the caricature like that of Muriel Porter amongst others—we must understand how he thought of the church systematically. With regards to God's work of redemption, Knox recognized a broader category describing the interrelation between persons and communities. We might call this category the 'people of God' or the 'redemptive community'—Knox himself did not specify. This category is analogous to what many have called the universal earthly church, but avoids conceptual inflation.[99] Knox restricted his theology of the church to what he saw in the biblical text, namely that the church is a gathering. In doing so, he believed the practice of the church would be sharper and more effective and not distracted or hindered by other inappropriate impositions.

---

[99] See Graham Cole, "The Doctrine of the Church: Towards Conceptual Clarification," in *Explorations 2: Church, Worship and the Local Congregation*, ed. B.G. Webb (Homebush, N.S.W.: Lancer, 1987), 3–17.

Therefore, with regards to church unity he believed that there will never be *visibly* one assembly before the Parousia; nowhere on earth is there the potential of physically gathering all Christians into one assembly. Earthly gatherings are physical; and if it cannot represent itself physically, it is not a church. The heavenly gathering, on the other hand, is spiritual, and therefore it is an object of faith; it remains unseen. True unity of all believers in an assembly only occurs at the eschaton (2 Thess. 2:1).

For Knox, both the unity and catholicity of the church are bound to the presence of Christ. Christ is the focal point of the church, the person around whom and for whom the people of God gather. Christ is not only the focal point, but the *cause* of the church; he himself is gathering people unto himself, as he himself is building the church (Matt. 16:18). Therefore, Christ guarantees the unity of the church. He is in one place and therefore he is only gathering one church. There is no potential for division or disunity. Knox wrote,

> The unity of the church springs from the unity of the relationship with Christ, which all believers have. They are all gathered in Christ's church in his presence round him in heaven. That is, they each experience the immediate presence of Christ which comes from being with him face to face through his Spirit present to their spirits. They talk with him, obey him, they are his friends, love him and love all his. The unity of the visible church consists of accepting into full membership of the congregation all true believers who happen to be in the congregation at the meeting of the congregation. It is Christ's church; he has gathered all its members. Every one who is Christ's and has been gathered by him is as true a member of that congregation or church ... Thus the unity of the heavenly church is expressed in the unity of the visible church by the complete acceptance into full fellowship of all who call upon the name of the Lord.[100]

Knox believed that because of the reality of the heavenly gathering, the earthly gathering possessed something actual. That is, the singular heavenly gathering gives expression in many local (earthly) congregations, and of which each is the full expression. The unity of the

---

[100] Knox, *Works*, II.94.

heavenly is guaranteed by the singular presence of Christ. Thus, the reciprocal presence we have already seen has bearing on issues pertaining to the unity of the church. The unity of the church is a reality, not a goal, as the heavenly church is united around Christ and his Spirit unites the earthly church in Christ.[101]

It is clear that Knox saw Christ as the guarantor of ecclesial unity. However, equally clear is his conviction that the means by which Christ affects this unity is by the Spirit.[102] The doctrine of the Spirit was critical as a presupposition for his doctrine of the church. The Spirit's work is particularly seen in the light of the biblical metaphor of the church as the 'body of Christ.' Knox understood that Christ is building his church, his body, of which he is the head. But in Christ's body, it is the Holy Spirit who draws people into this body, animates the body, and unifies it.[103] Knox wrote,

> We Christians are a body, created by the Holy Spirit who indwells each one of us. He indwells each part of the body and so brings it into a unity. The body metaphor is a perfect description of the Christian fellowship ... Christ is in each person in his Spirit. The one Spirit indwells each member and each acts in response to his guidance. The analogy between our physical body indwelt by our being and Christ's spiritual body indwelt by him is complete.[104]

---

[101] Knox believed that unity of the church was achieved at Pentecost when the Spirit descended upon the believers, and afterwards indwelt all believers henceforth. Knox wrote, 'This prayer of Jesus [for unity (John 17)] was answered on the day of Pentecost, when God's Spirit was given to the disciples and to all who believed in Jesus through their word. The Spirit of God unites Christians into a unity. The Spirit of God indwells each Christian heart. God is in them and they are in God, just as Jesus had prayed. No more real unity can be imagined. This unity has already been given to us and can never be dissolved, but we ought to give expression to it by our relationship to each other.' D. Broughton Knox, "Christian Unity," Protestant Faith radio broadcast 26 June 1977, published in ibid., II.35.
[102] D. Broughton Knox, "The Body of Christ," in ibid., II.38.
[103] Ibid., II.37–39.
[104] Ibid., II.67.

For Knox, there is a very close nexus between Jesus and his Spirit in ecclesiology, as is appropriate in orthodox Trinitarian theology. The presence of Christ in the life of believers is the presence of his Holy Spirit.[105] Furthermore, inherent within the body metaphor is an interaction amongst the parts of the body. The body metaphor highlights the *raison d'etre* of the church as fellowship.

Fellowship

While Knox did not see the earthly church extending beyond the local congregation, this did not mean he envisaged churches in isolation or autonomy. Knox located the church systematically in a broader category of *fellowship*. It is noteworthy that while this chapter concerns Knox's ecclesiology, theology proper was his great love. It is no surprise, then, that his ecclesiology was intimately connected to his doctrine of God. Knox believed that fellowship springs from the doctrine of God in the first instance, but is something God extends to his people in his saving activity. God's people participate in fellowship most intimately in the church context, but also more broadly in many other activities and networks. In this broader sense, churches express fellowship with other churches in networks aimed at common activities and mission. The most common expression of this ecclesial fellowship is seen in denominations, in which churches express their interdependence upon others. Knox maintained, however, that while these networks served the local churches and their common mission, they were not churches themselves in any institutional sense. This, of course, meant firm boundaries for what authority or coercion denominations could rightly express over congregations.

Knox defined fellowship as 'friends sharing a common activity or a common possession. It's not just friendship. It's friendship sharing something.'[106] Friendship is something that humans seek and experience with one another. Knox wrote, 'It is a relationship between persons who

---

[105] Demonstrating the nexus of Christology and Pneumatology, Knox wrote, 'Christ is the life of the body, that is, of Christians in fellowship. Jesus is the life of every individual, "Christ lives in me" (Gal 2:20) and he is the life of the group "Christ who is our life" (Col 3:4). There is a close parallel here to the notion of the Spirit. Just as life is in every part of our natural body, so Christ is in every part of his body. Since Christ is in each individual Christian, the Christian's body is also Christ's body and at the same time part of Christ's body.' ibid., II.39.
[106] D. Broughton Knox, "Acts 2:42," in ibid., II.52.

appreciate, have affection towards, and wish to advance the welfare of each other.'[107] Fellowship, then, is an extension of friendship. Knox explained, 'It is friendship expressed in joint endeavour, friends doing things together. It makes friendship even more enjoyable. It is the happiest human experience. Friendship implies possessing one another but fellowship implies possessing something else in addition. It is friends sharing a common possession leading to a common activity on the basis of that sharing.'[108] Fellowship, then, can happen among all people, Christian or not. However, the definitive mark of Christian fellowship is the possession that Christians share: the Holy Spirit, God himself.[109]

The wonder of Christian fellowship is that it extends beyond mere human relationships, to humans having fellowship with God himself (1 John 1:3). Knox continued,

> Our truest fellowship is the sharing of Christ. The fellowship of our Lord Jesus Christ is parallel to and indeed the same as the fellowship of the Spirit. ... But because the common possession in which we share is a person, it is not only sharing a possession but sharing a relationship. Our fellowship unites us all into one, with God the Father, Son and Holy Spirit and one with one another in Christ. We all should participate in mutual friendship and fellowship. God with us and we with God and with one another.[110]

Knox recognized that the fellowship that Christians enjoy, especially in gathering together, is in the Holy Spirit. This fellowship of the Christians is with other Christians and with the Triune God himself. The basis of Christian fellowship is the sacrifice of Jesus the Christ. This sacrifice enables horizontal reconciliation with other Christians, as well as vertical reconciliation with God.[111] Thus Christian fellowship is a mediated activity, grounded in the soteriological work of Christ applied by the Spirit. The mediation of Christ grants Christians constant access to the

---

[107] Ibid., II.57.
[108] Ibid., II.57–58.
[109] Ibid.
[110] Ibid., II.70.
[111] Ibid., II.41.

presence of the Trinity. Knox wrote, 'Christians are also always in God's company, in Christ's company, and in the Spirit's company. As Jesus promised, "If a man love me, he will keep my word; and the Father will love him, and we will come and make our home with him" (John 14:23). This promise is fulfilled by the Spirit's presence. The Christian is always in the presence of God as his friend.'[112] So, because of the work of Christ applied by the Spirit, Christians are constantly in fellowship with the triune God.

But if Christians are always in the presence of the Trinity spiritually, why must they gather for the sake of experiencing this presence (Matthew 18:20)? Is there an experiential reality that is reserved for the corporate gathering? The presence of Christ, by his Spirit, finds its expression most naturally in the presence of other Christians. Christians gather together on earth to experience not only the joy of each other's company, but the presence of the Spirit of God in the lives of other believers. This recognition of Knox is similar to what is taught in 1 John, though Knox did not identify this truth with that text specifically. In 1 John 3:16, the Apostle identifies the love of God with the giving over of the Son unto death. Then in 1 John 4:7-23, John articulates that love is known by the Spirit. He even says that God is invisible, but that He is made visible in the love of Christians for one another (1 Jn 4:12-13). Such is it to abide in love by the Spirit. Therefore, the fellowship that Christians enjoy with one another is intricately connected to the fellowship they enjoy with the triune God.

With more specific reference to the church, Christian fellowship is experienced more frequently and is a broader concept than the *ekklēsia,* as it occurs beyond the gathering; however, it is not less than the *ekklēsia*. The local church is essential to the Christian experience of fellowship, both with other Christians and with the Trinity. Knox believed that the church is essentially fellowship. He expressed both the vertical and horizontal aspects of fellowship in what he called 'fellowship in God.' Indispensable to this fellowship in God is the Word of God. Knox wrote, 'The Christian church is nothing else than fellowship in God, and this fellowship is deepened and maintained by the teaching of the word of God by the minister. Without this teaching there can be no fellowship,

---

[112] Ibid., II.63–64.

that is, no church.'[113] The Word of God is the substance around which the church has fellowship. It is also through the proclamation of the Word of God that Christians are called into faith. The church is a creature of the Word.

Denominations?

As we have seen, Knox's view is that on earth there is no ecclesial reality beyond the local church—but there *is* a broader experience of Christian fellowship between churches that extends beyond the local gathering. The most common expression of this fellowship between congregations is in a denomination, in which churches unite in common conviction and cause. Knox believed that fellowship is required for health in both the individual Christian life and the corporate life of the church. Having fellowship beyond the local congregation is a reminder that Christians belong to the larger heavenly church.[114]

Knox stressed the interdependency of Christians and churches that is expressed in fellowship. He wrote,

> Independency is not a Christian concept. It is contrary to God's nature, and to our nature as he has created it. Independency is a contradiction of Christian fellowship. Congregations should not act without respect to other congregations. Denominational structures assist the interdependence of congregations. These links are a natural creation of the fellowship of the Spirit of God. The denomination and its officers have a ministry which is common to all Christians, that is to help, advise, encourage and exhort the congregation and its members.[115]

Knox emphasized the value of denominations in a manner that appears disproportionate to his understanding of the nature of the church. This feature of his work is surprising, as congregational independence would at least appear to be the most reasonable conclusion to his theology. But his understanding of fellowship constrains him from permitting this

---

[113] D. Broughton Knox, "The Priority of Preaching: Prepare and Preach Properly or Perish," in ibid., II.241.
[114] Ibid., II.95–96.
[115] Ibid., II.98.

separation. He argued that independency is not a Christian concept, but he did not corroborate this claim with reference to Scripture. Perhaps he had in mind the interdependence of congregations in the New Testament, especially for the sake of missionary tasks and the guarding of doctrine (e.g. Acts 15, Rom. 15).

Greater clarity concerning Knox's view of denominations is achieved when it is understood in relation to the broader conceptual framework that he outlined. Denominations belong in the conceptual category of fellowship, not ecclesiology. The church is *not* an institution. He wrote,

> The doctrine of the church has no place within it for denominations. These are like missionary societies, being expressions of Christian fellowship, and the ministries of their office bearers are helping ministries to facilitate those whom Christ has built into his church to express their fellowship with Christ the better, both in their local church and as his witnesses and servants in the world.[116]

Knox believed that denominations are helpful for congregations, but was careful to stress that the local church is *the* church on earth. No larger group of churches, no matter what extent of fellowship they share, is a church, since a church implies gathering. Knox preferred to think of denominations as parachurch organizations, existing alongside local churches to aid in fellowship.[117] He wrote,

> Denominations are called "churches", and this nomenclature misleads many into thinking that they are part of the one holy catholic apostolic church. But the denomination is not a church, inasmuch as the denomination never gathers. Gathering is the only meaning of the word "church" in the Old and New Testaments ... The denomination is an organizational structure to facilitate the fellowship of the church with Christians in other churches. To call the denomination a church is strictly inaccurate, and in furtherance of clarity

---

[116] Ibid.
[117] Ibid., II.95.

of thought ought to be dropped, and the word "denomination" always substituted.[118]

Denominations function as service structures for the local church, with the purpose of helping other churches to join in fellowship. The purpose of this fellowship is to facilitate a range of ministries such as mission and theological education that a local church could not carry out alone in the same capacity. However, it is crucial for the denomination not to overstep its bounds. It is not designed to *surpass* congregations, but rather to *support* local congregations. [119] The displacement of the authority of the local church for the sake of denominational dominance is an error that has subverted much local church viability. The end of these organizations has been misunderstood; the *telos* is not the institution, but the congregation.[120] The denomination is not the church, but a support agency for it.[121]

One of the louder voices of criticism of Knox's ecclesiology, and that of his successors, is Muriel Porter. She has taken particular issue with the implications of Knox's conclusions for the broader denomination, especially the 'national' church. She believes that '[t]he

---

[118] Ibid., II.96.

[119] For more on the danger of denominations and the necessary correctives, see ibid., II.31.

[120] In one instance, Knox cautioned against misplaced allegiance due to misunderstanding the end. Knox wrote, "Perhaps the most serious danger which the denominational groupings of Christian congregations presents is that such groupings provide a focal point for loyalty. For many members, especially for the more carnal members, the denomination replaces the true centre of loyalty which a Christian assembly should have, namely Christ who gathers his assembly together. Thus nowadays we witness Christians assembling, both locally and on a world-wide scale, on the ground of their denominational allegiance, and the issue is confused by the fact that invariably the denominations is called 'the church,' as though Christ who assembles his church were also the one who is assembling the denominational gathering." D. Broughton Knox, *Sent by Jesus: Some Aspects of Christian Ministry Today* (Edinburgh: Banner of Truth, 1992). 61.

[121] For a clear exposition and application of Knox's views on denominations see Mark D. Thompson, "The Church of God and the Anglican Church of Australia," in *'Wonderfully and Confessedly Strange': Australian Essays in Anglican Ecclesiology*, ed. Bruce Kaye (Adelaide: ATF Press, 2006), 237–242.

national church in this scenario, is little more than an administrative arrangement, the expectations and statutory obligations of which can legitimately be challenged and even avoided.'[122] Her contention is that Sydney Diocese has only kept to their constitutional obligations and not progressed with the broader 'church' culture beyond the 1961 constitution to grant more authority to the Primate.[123] Likewise, she is displeased that Sydney Diocese withdrew funding in support of the Lambeth Conference in 2008—a move that she does not acknowledge was done by *many* others in the Anglican communion in protest to the support of same-sex practice in the church.[124] Strangely, she does not ever cite the work of Knox and challenge his ecclesiology theologically. Her rhetoric is highly emotive and politically charged.

By Porter's own admission, Sydney Diocese has kept the law according to the church constitution (1961). In fact, it was Knox who, with others, pushed for many reforms to that constitution.[125] We have demonstrated above that Knox was ideologically favourable to denominational fellowship. But, he was adamant that the denomination is not the church. Therefore, the authority of the denomination ought not to be understood as ecclesial authority. What Knox did not specify was how the local church ought to conceive of its participation in the denomination. What he did make clear was the good that was to come of the fellowship in the denomination, namely joint ventures in mission, theological education, and preservation of doctrine. When the denomination fails the local church at these levels—such as assigning funding to institutional bolstering or embracing doctrine counter to biblical truth and the Reformed heritage of the denomination—then the local church and its close networks of fellowship should not be obliged to participate. The difference between Knox's position (and that of his successors) and Porter's is ecclesiology and the location of authority. Porter believes the church is an institution and authority rests with the denominational leaders. For Knox, the church is the congregation and the authority is the Bible over the congregation.

Knox's conclusions regarding the unity of the church, fellowship and denominations also have considerable implications for the

---

[122] Porter, *Sydney Anglicans*, 77.
[123] Ibid., 78.
[124] Ibid., 79.
[125] See Kuhn, *Ecclesiology of Robinson and Knox*, 41–46.

ecumenical movement as seen in efforts of the World Council of Churches (WCC). Knox himself participated at the WCC as a delegate for several meetings. Knox believed that local church unity is the only earthly unity to be sought, as the local church is the only earthly ecclesial reality. Ultimately, from Knox's perspective, the mistake of the WCC was the confusion of the heavenly and earthly church. That is, the WCC ascribed properties of the heavenly church to the earthly church, namely catholicity. But the earthly church is incapable of catholicity, as a catholic gathering cannot and does not occur. Thus, seeking unity amongst catholicity is a pointless task. Catholicity only exists in heaven; therefore, catholic unity is only seen and realized *in* heaven. As the church is only local on earth, the unity of the church is expressed in the local congregation.

Conclusion

We have sought to address the question, 'Was D.B. Knox a congregationalist?' We have answered in the affirmative with the support of the following key points from his ecclesiology: The *ekklēsia* is a gathering, and the Christian *ekklēsia* is the gathering of believers around Christ. However, the *ekklēsia* is primarily a heavenly reality, gathered around Christ where he is. The heavenly finds physical expression of its spiritual reality in the local assembly, which is a full representation of the heavenly church and is gathered by the Holy Spirit. The local assembly gathers for fellowship, as it gathers to encounter Christ. This encounter is spiritual as believers encounter the Spirit of Christ in each other. The distinguishing mark of Christian fellowship is the Word of God. As the congregation is the only legitimate church on earth, there is no institutional authority naturally set over the local church. However, the local church should maintain fellowship with other churches, even in an institutional (denominational) framework.

To conclude, we offer one polemical note, as well as an appraisal of Knox's ecclesiology; these will be one in the same. One of the strongest critiques of Knox's congregational ecclesiology has come through Muriel Porter's identification of Knox's influence on his successors and the detrimental consequences of his theology upon Sydney Diocese's position within the wider Anglican communion. While Knox and Sydney Anglicans after him have not capitulated to the broader agenda and demands of the Anglican Church in Australia, nor have they sanctioned the liberal agenda of much of the wider Anglican Church, they have sought broad reaching fellowship for renewal and reform around the globe. One could hardly accuse Sydney Diocese of parochialism, or mere tribalism, unless the tribe is broadly understood as Reformed Protestantism of the Evangelical kind. While Knox's theology of church may be congregational, it is not to the detriment of wider fellowship. This congregational understanding of the church is anchored in biblical theological convictions that seek to uphold the primacy of Word ministry. This ministry, when flourishing, promotes wonderfully rich fellowship for the sake of gospel mission.

Sacramentology: Was Knox Really Anti-Sacraments?

Edward Loane

I was recently asked my opinion about what topics might be relevant for a conference in Sydney focusing on the challenge of the Reformation for today. In particular, the organiser wanted to focus on some reformation doctrines that were under threat at the moment. The obvious challenges to justification and the authority of Scripture came to mind, but I also suggested they might be well served by thinking about the doctrine of the sacraments. This was a touchstone issue for the Reformers, especially in the Anglican tradition. Indeed, many lost their lives because of their sacramental convictions. Considering this, I have often wondered what they would make of contemporary evangelical practice and I thought an exploration of this issue would be searching and challenging at a conference of contemporary church workers. The organiser of the conference agreed that the sacraments were a big issue for the Reformers, but he felt it would be too hot a topic for a contemporary conference. Perhaps endorsing the Reformers' convictions about this doctrine might lead the contemporary evangelical to being burnt at the stake! Contemporary Sydney ministers, it seems, are radically divided over this issue. A number firmly believe the doctrine and practice expressed in the 39 Articles and Prayer Book are unbiblical. Others are convinced that the opposite is true. Perhaps most are quite apathetic to the place of sacraments in the life of the church. They just do not care one way or another about sacraments.

How did this situation come about? Is Broughton Knox responsible? There is no doubt Knox was immensely influential on Sydney Anglicanism—what was his understanding of the sacraments? Was he anti-sacraments?

Certainly, it has been postulated that Knox's theology diminished the traditional place the sacraments have had in the Anglican Church. Murial Porter linked Knox's position with Sydney Diocese's exploration towards lay presidency. She stated that 'By the 1970s, Broughton Knox's teaching on revelation as anti-sacramental and the ordained ministry as primarily a preaching role was bearing fruit.'[126] The influence of Knox against sacraments is similarly raised in Marcia Cameron's biography of Knox. She summarises his work *New Testament Baptism* and concludes that the consequence of his view 'is the downgrading of the rite of water baptism.' She goes on to say that 'there was no urging to partake in this sacrament of the Anglican Church' and 'some of Broughton's disciples might well have concluded that the ceremony was unimportant.'[127]

These comments open up for us two other related and important questions in the evaluation of Knox's position. Firstly, we must acknowledge the dynamic nature and development of a person's theology. What Knox expressed in the 1960s may not have been rearticulated in the early 1990s because of a change in emphasis or indeed trajectory in his thinking. Which position is most representative and most influential? The second issue is the question of sources. On the issue of Knox's theology of the Lord's Supper and Baptism we have several relevant items. On the one hand, we have published books like his 1967 *Thirty-Nine Articles* which was revised in 1976 and his 1983 *The Lord's Supper from Wycliffe to Cranmer*. These works were obviously subject to substantial reflection and were exposed to serious editorial consideration before publication. On the other hand, the collection of Knox's *Selected Works* provides a wide range of previously unpublished sources often with limited details regarding the context and date of the writing. This collection is a wonderful resource and, at the same time, a challenge for the historical theologian. How should the evidence be weighed? The *Selected Works* includes a single page 'Note on the Lord's Supper' from 1992 and a double page 'A Short Statement on the Lord's Supper' which is undated. Although the context for both is unclear, to me these read a little like something a minister would say to introduce the communion service on a Sunday. In other words, this is a very different kind of source to his previously published works on the subject. Both are valuable in our assessment, but we must be careful not to place more weight on the theological emphasis of a brief 'Note' than is warranted.

I will just make one further preliminary comment before we address the topic at hand. Broughton Knox was my great uncle and he

---

[126] Porter, *Sydney Anglicans*, 98.
[127] Marcia Cameron, *An Enigmatic Life: David Broughton Knox: Father of Contemporary Sydney Anglicanism* (Brunswick East, Vic: Acorn Press, 2006). 223–224.

died in my early teens. I remember personal interactions with him in my childhood, but it is not a surprise that I cannot remember ever speaking with him about his sacramental theology! The reason I mention this is because there are many still living (and perhaps reading this chapter) who have firsthand recollections of Knox's teaching on this. I am sure there are many anecdotes and reminiscences that could be shared about what he said about this issue or taught in class on that issue; however, I am limiting my analysis to what has been published. The evaluation will begin by investigating Knox's writing on sacraments in general and will then focus on what he says about the Lord's Supper and baptism. This study will allow us to provide an assessment of whether he was 'anti-sacraments'.

Knox on Sacraments

In a number of his writings Knox makes clear what his understanding of the sacraments is. He says, 'The word "sacrament" is a synonym for the word "sign" and the one word may be substituted for the other without any change in meaning.'[128] Indeed, he claims that 'the Reformers always used the word sacrament to mean sign'.[129] Knox argued that it is important not to equate the thing signified with the sign itself for to do so would 'annihilate the sign which the Lord appointed, and overthrow the nature of the sacrament.'[130] At this point it is important to note that in this statement Knox affirmed the sacraments were given by the Lord. Furthermore, he was happy to describe them as 'effectual signs' when 'accompanied by the explanatory word'.[131] Their efficacy is twofold. First, they convey the message of forgiveness and incorporation into Christ. Second, 'they are the means of bringing the promised blessing to those who believe and who express their faith in the promise by using its signs.'[132] Knox was unashamed to claim that the sacraments 'go beyond the word' because they impressed the promises of God on our minds 'not

---

[128] Knox, *Thirty-Nine Articles (2nd ed.)*.

[129] D. Broughton Knox, *The Lord's Supper from Wycliffe to Cranmer* (Exeter: Paternoster, 1983). 40.

[130] "A Short Statement on the Lord's Supper (Date unknown)" in Knox, *Works*, II.317.

[131] D. Broughton Knox, *The Thirty-Nine Articles: The Historic Basis of Anglican Faith*, 1st ed. (London: Hodder and Stoughton, 1967). 38.

[132] Ibid.

merely by the sense of hearing but by sight and touch' and because of this they 'fortify faith'.[133] He described the sacraments as '*seals* which confirm the promise in our consciousness'.[134]

One of the key issues Knox sought to address was a wrong understanding of the sacraments. He claimed that they can easily be 'misinterpreted as religious works, by doing which the sinner obtains grace from God'. As such, he commends the Thirty-Nine Articles for defining the sacraments as 'God's word to us' because the 'acted word of the sacraments' functions in the same way as the written word of Scripture, namely, 'it is faith in God and in his promise which brings the blessing promised, whether it be salvation or any other gift'.[135] Nevertheless, while wanting to protect believers from potential misunderstandings relating to sacraments, Knox unambiguously affirmed their value. He stated, 'The sacraments are God's sacraments, God's gracious words of promise to us. Through them God holds out to us everlasting life in Christ.'[136] Indeed he illustrated his understanding of the sacraments with the analogy of deeds of conveyance. (Those who are familiar with his priorities for Moore College growth in property assets may be unsurprised by this analogy coming to his mind).[137] He made the point that in one sense, the deeds are paper and ink—they are not the property itself. However, they are not *merely* paper and ink or *merely* reminders of the property. The person who receives them receives the property... 'on one important condition: he must be the duly qualified person to receive them, otherwise the deeds convey nothing to him'.[138] Knox concludes, 'the sacraments convey eternal life by way of promise to those (and only to those) who perceive and believe that promise.'[139]

This is a strong statement about the sacraments, but it is repeated in Knox's writings. For example, in his pamphlet entitled *Justification By Faith* he turns his attention to why the New Testament speaks of the sacraments bringing forgiveness and participation in Christ if works have

---

[133] Ibid.
[134] Ibid.
[135] Ibid., 36.
[136] Ibid., 37.
[137] See chapter 6 by Mark Thompson for more details.
[138] Knox, *Thirty-Nine Articles (1st ed.)*, 37.
[139] Ibid.

no part in justification. His answer is that the sacraments 'are nothing other than faith expressed in action'.[140] They are means of taking hold by faith the promises of God and thus they save. Knox maintained that in *both* sacraments God holds out for acceptance His promises and by them the Gospel is preached and its benefits appropriated.[141] Both the promises and the response of faith are embodied in the actions. Furthermore, he stated that 'as the expression of faith, [the sacraments] may properly be said to save, and are so spoken of in the New Testament.'[142] Drawing this teaching together we may offer a preliminary conclusion that Knox maintained a Reformed doctrine of the sacraments which valued them highly and cherished their place in the church. However, we may need to modify this conclusion as we come to study Knox's teaching on the individual sacraments because, as we do so, we observe a more idiosyncratic position than is traditionally associated with Reformed theology.

Knox on the Lord's Supper

If we turn first to Knox's understanding of the Lord's Supper, we note a number of important features. He was unambiguous that the Lord's Supper was the preaching of the gospel and its appropriation when the believer receives in faith. He said, 'The soul feeds on Christ, the living bread.'[143] In contradistinction to the Roman Catholic doctrine he stated, 'Christ is not in the bread and wine but he dwells in our heart by faith'.[144] Such statements certainly resonate with the reformed Anglican tradition.

One of the interesting things I noted in my research for this chapter was the differences in the 1967 edition and the 1976 edition of *Thirty-Nine Articles*. In the earlier edition, Knox's commentary on the Articles moves from discussing 'Sacraments and the Church' to 'The Doctrine of Ministry'. In the later edition, he inserts a section on 'The Lord's Supper'. This interlude is interesting as, in stark contrast to the sections from the earlier edition, commentary on the Articles is almost

---

[140] D. Broughton Knox, *Justification by Faith* (Sydney: Church Book Room, 1983 [1959]). 17.
[141] Ibid.
[142] Ibid., 18.
[143] Ibid.
[144] Knox, *Works*, II.410.

entirely abandoned.[145] Rather, he takes his reader on an excursus into a topic that will become prominent in his writing on the Lord's Supper in later years. He emphasised the Lord's Supper as 'fellowship with the Lord and one another in the presence of the Lord'.[146] In fact, this inserted section is almost identical to the section that the Matthias Media volume has printed separately as an undated 'Short Note on the Lord's Supper'.[147] In this section, Knox wrote that 'in this fellowship we proclaim the great fact of his saving death…'.[148] The element of proclamation is significant. In his 'Notes on the Lord's Supper' he highlighted the importance of this aspect when he wrote '[God] speaks to us, through his word remembered, read, and preached from the pulpit, but particularly preached from the holy table, that is when we are truly instructed.'[149] A comment like this appears very strong. So does his assertion a few lines earlier that 'The Lord's Supper was given to us by Jesus to remember Jesus. *It has no other purpose.*'[150] As I noted earlier, if we could know the context of these claims—whether a church service, a lecture or just some random thoughts jotted down—we would be aided in our assessment of how accurately they reflected Knox's considered opinion.

Nevertheless, Knox's emphasis on fellowship should not be underestimated. He claimed 'The grace (that is, the gift or benefit from God) of this sacrament is fellowship with Christ in the Spirit on the basis of the forgiveness of our sins. No greater grace, gift or benefit is possible in this life…'[151] In his work on *The Lord's Supper from Wycliffe to Cranmer*, Knox reiterated his point that the sacrament was fundamentally about fellowship. He championed Wycliffe as 'the first Englishman to teach clearly and fully the Reformed doctrine of the Lord's Supper'.[152] In fact, he claimed that Wycliffe was 'nearer to the truth' than later Reformed theology because 'he understood the Lord's Supper as a sign of

---

[145] There is one reference to Article 29 in the second last sentence of the three-page section.

[146] Knox, *Thirty-Nine Articles (2nd ed.)*, 33.

[147] Knox, *Works*, II.317–318.

[148] Knox, *Thirty-Nine Articles (2nd ed.)*, 33.

[149] Knox, *Works*, II.319.

[150] Ibid. Italics mine.

[151] Knox, *Thirty-Nine Articles (2nd ed.)*, 35.

[152] Knox, *Lord's Supper from Wycliffe to Cranmer*, 9.

fellowship'.[153] This was the reason why, according to Knox, Wycliffe insisted the piety of the minister affected the efficacy of the sacrament. Apart from the reformer George Joye, 'the character of the Lord's Supper as fellowship was not a concept stressed by other English Reformers'.[154] In this work, Knox maintained that it is not the sign that is the purpose of the Lord's Supper but the activity which is 'the true centre'.[155] The activity is fellowship. The sign is the word of the gospel that is the basis of the fellowship. Faith in the word is the response which is itself the fellowship with Christ, and so with one another in Christ.[156] For Knox, this overcame the conundrum of justifying the supper over and against the word as 'fellowship is an end in itself'.[157]

As we have seen, Knox's understanding of the Lord's Supper, and particularly his emphasis on the Lord's Supper as fellowship, cannot be construed as anti-sacramental. If anything, clearly articulating the purpose of fellowship in Lords Supper provides further grounds for the sacrament rather than undermining it.

Knox on Baptism

Now we shall turn our attention to Knox's understanding of baptism which is, I believe, somewhat more problematic. If we stuck to his published *Thirty-Nine Articles* we would find him affirming that Baptism is a 'visible sign' of 'the promises of the forgiveness of sin, and of our adoption to be the sons of God by the Holy Ghost' (Article 27).[158] However, probably more controversial was his unpublished paper which was later published in the *Selected Works* called *New Testament Baptism*. This work seeks to systematically analyse the New Testament data on baptism to determine its meaning and place in early Christian practice. It is worth spending some time critically evaluating Knox's argument and exegesis in our assessment of his sacramental theology. As we shall see, he certainly arrives at novel conclusions in relation to the place of water baptism in the apostolic tradition.

---

[153] Ibid., 19.
[154] Ibid., 37.
[155] Ibid., 41.
[156] Ibid.
[157] Ibid.
[158] Knox, *Thirty-Nine Articles (1st ed.)*, 37.

Knox begins his argument by claiming that 'There is no other doctrine or practice in which differences of opinion are so diverse among Christians who hold that the Bible is the source of what they should believe on Christian matters!'[159] The aim of his work was to investigate whether 'traditional Christian views on baptism' corresponded with the New Testament teaching. Even at this point, we note a little contradiction in his logic. He began by stating that 'there is no agreement among [Christians] about what baptism means, or what its result is, or how it should be administered...' but then seeks to assess 'the traditional views' on the subject. This is a minor inconsistency in the scheme of things, but it demonstrates the tone of the work as primarily polemic and lacking nuance. It is obviously a work that had not been submitted to peer review associated with the publication process.

In looking at the New Testament teaching, Knox starts with John's Baptism. He argued that John's message was primarily one of repentance and baptism showed his followers' determination to change their way of life. This 'once-off' washing was different to the repeated washings established in the Levitical system. Knox claimed that 'Jewish proselyte baptism is more likely to have been copied from John rather than vice versa' and references the fact that, according to Beasley-Murray, the first indisputable reference to Jewish proselyte baptism belongs to the end of the first century.[160] In fact, Beasley-Murray is more circumspect in his conclusions, stating,

> The question of whether Jewish proselyte baptism was historically antecedent to the ministries of John the Baptist and Jesus, and if so the extent to which it influenced the Christian rite, are extraordinarily difficult to answer with any degree of confidence.[161]

Indeed, Beasley-Murray's conclusion is that Jewish proselyte baptism was probably practiced prior to Christian baptism.[162] Knox, however, goes on to argue that John based his physical baptising on the metaphorical uses of washing meaning repentance in the Old Testament such as in Isaiah

---

[159] Knox, *Works*, II.263.
[160] Ibid., II.264.
[161] G.P. Beasley-Murray, *Baptism in the New Testament* (London: Macmillan and Co, 1962). 18.
[162] Ibid., 31.

1:16-17 and Jeremiah 4:14. Knox believed that this metaphor of washing to describe repentance continued to be used by New Testament authors such as in James 4:8 and 1 Corinthians 6:11. He claimed that the common passive translation of 1 Corinthians 6:11 'you were washed' is incorrect because the Greek verb form is middle tense. He believed it should be translated 'you washed yourself' and was essentially another way of saying you repented. In Daniel Wallace's *Greek Grammar Beyond the Basics*, however, he shows that there are several ways the middle tense is used and he classes this as a 'permissive middle', meaning 'you allowed yourselves to be washed'. As such, the simple passive 'you were washed' captures the meaning.[163] Knox goes on to make a similar claim about Ananias' words to Paul, claiming '"be baptised" is an incorrect translation'.[164] It should be translated, according to Knox, 'baptise yourself', which indicates repentance was in view. This interpretation of the middle tense is at odds with the parallel account of these events in Acts 9:18 which simply uses the passive form of the verb that Paul 'was baptised'. Again, Wallace classes the use of the middle voice in Acts 22:16 as a permissive middle form of the verb meaning 'have yourself baptised'.[165] This may seem a pedantic issue, but Knox's idiosyncratic translation of these two verses is foundational for the remainder of his argument so it is worth highlighting the issue. Knox argued that in many places the meaning of the word baptism is simply shorthand for repentance and does not refer to water baptism at all. He claimed that not translating the verbs in 1 Corinthians 6 and Acts 22 as he did—which is the case in every significant English version of the Bible—was 'an example of the misunderstanding of the symbolism of water baptism'.[166] However, if we are to follow Wallace and the English translations of these verses we see that allowing yourself to be washed/baptised has much clearer resonance with water baptism and this undermines Knox's thesis that this was simply a metaphor for repentance.

---

[163] Daniel B. Wallace, *Greek Grammar: Beyond the Basics* (Grand Rapids: Zondervan, 1996). 427.
[164] Knox, *Works*, II.265.
[165] Wallace, *Greek Grammar*, 426.
[166] f/n 3 Knox, *Works*, II.265.

Knox's argument proceeded by using his (novel) understanding of the middle voice in Acts 22:16 as a hermeneutical guide for other New Testament passages. For example, he stated:

> when Peter was asked by the Jerusalem crowd what it should do in view of what it had heard in his sermon, he replied "Repent and be baptized, in the name of Jesus Christ, with a view to the forgiveness of your sins" (Acts 2:38). Here "repent and be baptized" is a hendiadys, that is, the use of two words to refer to one thing.[167]

This is a very strong claim in relation to this passage. Just a few verses later those who received Peter's word were baptized (Acts 2:41). As such, the context would point to Peter, rather than using two words to mean the same thing, speaking of two related actions: repent and be baptised with water. Nevertheless, following Knox's claim that Peter's use of 'repent and be baptized' in Acts 2:38 was two words referring to one thing, he goes on to state that for John and the apostles water baptism was the sign that the believers had repented.[168] As he put it:

> When the gospel was preached from the day of Pentecost onwards, the apostles, many if not most of whom had been actively associated with John, continued baptism as a sign of repentance and of believing the messianic message and of being members of the messianic group awaiting the manifesting of the kingdom or rule of God.[169]

For Knox, the New Testament demonstrated that baptism's primary meaning was that of repentance, but its secondary meaning was to be a member of a group or a disciple of a leader. It had a personal aspect and a corporate aspect. Knox maintained that this secondary meaning was 'derivative' and he gave examples from 1 Corinthians 10:2, John 4:1-2, Acts 19:1-7 and 1 Corinthians 1:13 to demonstrate the New Testament use of baptism in this sense. In Acts 10, when the gentile Cornelius was converted and Peter said 'Surely no one can forbid the water that these should not be baptized', Knox stated that what he was really meaning was

---

[167] Ibid.
[168] Ibid., II.266.
[169] Ibid., II.266–267.

'Can anyone object to these people being full members of our group of believers?'[170] Furthermore, Knox stated that this baptism 'was followed by a much more significant indication. He shared a meal with them...'[171]

The argument of *New Testament Baptism* then goes on to assess the implications of Jesus' baptism by John. Knox claimed that Jesus' baptism 'does not figure prominently in the narratives' of the gospels and concludes that 'these writers saw no theological significance in Jesus' baptism, and this is confirmed by the fact that it apparently played no part in the theology of the New Testament Christians nor contributed to their theology of baptism'.[172] This is quite a remarkable claim. Knox says that John's gospel does not mention Jesus' baptism, which is strictly true. Although, John the Baptist does speak of seeing the Spirit coming upon Jesus as a dove, which according to the synoptics happened at Jesus' baptism (Matt 3:16, Mark 1:10, Luke 3:22). Each of the synoptic writers explicitly include the account of Jesus' baptism immediately prior to the declaration from heaven of Jesus' identity and this is followed by Jesus' temptation. The theological import that Jesus is God's promised messiah who identifies with sinners in baptism but does not sin is apparent. In Matthew's account Jesus points out the importance of his baptism by saying it was done 'to fulfil all righteousness' (Matt 3:15). These facts undermine Knox's contention that the baptism accounts are somewhat superfluous to the narrative and bear no theological significance for the writers.

Nevertheless, Knox's point is that Jesus' baptism did not change the meaning for Christians, it meant the same thing as it did for John: it was 'a baptism of discipleship'.[173] Knox maintained that this was appropriate,

> ...for at that time John was the leader. When the providence of God removed John from the leadership through Herod shutting him up in prison, then Jesus took over the leadership, preaching the same gospel. However it would seem that he dropped the rite of baptizing with

---

[170] Ibid., II.268.
[171] Ibid.
[172] Ibid., II.269.
[173] Ibid., II.270.

water, though his disciples revived it on the day of Pentecost.[174]

After Pentecost, the apostles continued to baptise with water. Knox stated that Paul administered water baptism to some of his converts but that he did not regard this as part of his apostolic ministry (1 Cor 1:15-16) and he concludes that 'John's custom of water baptism was still being continued by the members of the messianic movement but it is plain that its greatest proponent [Paul], like his Lord, did not set much on this water rite.'[175] Indeed, Knox went on to claim that while baptism was a legitimate gesture to express one's repentance, in itself it 'had no inherent relationship to the gospel'.[176] This is an extremely tenuous conclusion to draw from the New Testament teaching on baptism. It certainly must discount Paul's teaching in Romans 6:3-4, along with the other biblical evidence about the nature of baptism. When discussing the Ethiopian's baptism in Acts 8, Knox made the claim that his baptism was an expression of his faith and his changed mind and life. It was also his identification with other believers who were waiting for the coming of the kingdom.[177] Contrary to his previous conclusions, Knox's own claims about what water baptism meant for the Ethiopian do imply an inherent relationship between water baptism and the gospel.

In the next section of Knox's work he argued that in Paul's teaching there is a shift in his meaning of the use of the word 'baptism' towards a metaphorical meaning. He claims that water fades into the background as the theology of the New Testament develops. This, he maintained, derives from the 'fully metaphorical use of the concept of baptizing as discipling is in Jesus' last words to his apostles in Matthew 28'.[178] When Jesus refers to 'baptising them' in the great commission, Knox stated that this has 'no reference to the administering of water baptism'.[179] On the contrary, he wrote that Jesus consistently used the word 'baptism' and 'baptize' in a purely metaphorical sense, including when he spoke about baptism of the Holy Spirit. For Knox, Paul's claim

---

[174] Ibid.
[175] Ibid., II.272.
[176] Ibid., II.273.
[177] Ibid., II.277.
[178] Ibid., II.278.
[179] Ibid.

in 1 Corinthians 1 that he was not sent to baptize demonstrated that 'He regarded water baptism as of no importance'.[180] Again, this conclusion is not warranted from the text, especially considering what Knox had previously maintained about water baptism being the mark of belonging. In the context of Paul's statements to the Corinthians encouraging unity in Christ rather than the disunity of partisan association with different leaders, Paul asks the question, 'were you baptised into the name of Paul?' (1 Cor 1:13). The fact that Paul does not remember exactly who he baptised several years earlier does not necessarily imply 'he regarded water baptism as of no importance' as Knox asserted. On the contrary, the fact that he acknowledges administering water baptism and points to the fact it was in the name of Christ highlights the fact that it did have a significant place in his ministry and in the wider practice in the early church.

Knox argued that the New Testament strongly contrasts the water baptism of John and the promised Spirit baptism of the one following John. 'When John the Baptist coined the concept "baptised with the Spirit" it was entirely metaphorical, in sharp contrast with his literal water baptism.'[181] While, in many ways, Knox's comment about the metaphorical use of the word baptism in this spiritual sense is correct, we should be careful not to think that 'merely' metaphorical usage of a word means that something is not real, effective and has no correspondence with the literal usage. His use of the term *sharp contrast* throughout this work is unhelpful. As is his claim that this metaphorical use was 'with no relationship or reference to water baptism, except that of sharp contrast'.[182] It appears Knox has misunderstood the nature of metaphorical use. A metaphor is the application of a word to an object or action to which it does not literally apply, but to which it corresponds in some degree so as to render a representative or symbolic significance. Colin Gunton has shown how there is a tendency in rationalistic theology to downplay doctrine deriving from metaphors while they are still dependent upon the images that are their sources.[183] He goes on to argue that the difference between literal and metaphorical is fundamentally about use of a word in discourse but, as a result, 'there can be no absolute

---

[180] Ibid., II.281.
[181] Ibid., II.287.
[182] Ibid., II.283.
[183] Colin E Gunton, *The Actuality of Atonement: A Study of Metaphor, Rationality and the Christian Tradition* (Edinburgh: T&T Clarke, 1988). 18.

distinction between the literal and the metaphorical because the same word is sometimes one, sometimes the other.'[184] Thus, Knox's presentation of the 'sharp contrast' between the literal and metaphorical use of baptism with no relationship between them fails to adequately do justice to the purpose of employing a metaphor to convey this truth. The reason a metaphor is employed in the first place is because of the significant points of contact between the literal and the spiritual.

The danger of Knox's articulation and 'strong contrast' between literal water baptism and metaphorical spiritual baptism is that the two may be perceived to be at odds with one another. At this point it is worth contesting whether the metaphorical nature of Spiritual baptism is antagonistic to the cleansing that takes place in water baptism. Indeed, there is an important relationship between the symbol and the thing symbolised both in the word and the action. The Bible points to an actual spiritual 'cleansing' taking place in the life of the believer, washing away the defilement of sin and this is related to the symbolic act of baptism. For example, in Acts 22:16 Paul recounts that Ananias told him to 'Get up, be baptised and wash your sin away, calling on his name'. In other words, there is a genuine sense in which sins are 'washed away'. It is not that the metaphor is the antithesis of the reality, but it speaks truly of the reality. Likewise, in Titus 3:5 Paul speaks about salvation coming through 'the washing of regeneration and renewal of the Holy Spirit, whom he poured out on us richly through Jesus Christ our Saviour'. This is a passage which adopts the language of baptism to describe the experience of conversion and the metaphor is not divorced from a spiritual reality but describes it.

In 1 Corinthians 12:13 Paul claims that in one Spirit we were all baptized into one body. Knox used this verse, which goes on to state that we were all made to drink of the one Spirit, to argue that the baptism Paul is referring to is metaphorical rather than literal water baptism.[185] In the context, Paul is arguing for the unity of the church, but it is interesting that he points to the spiritual and baptismal reality to point to that unity. As such, we should be cautious about severing the relationship between the Spiritual and the physical which could be an implication of Knox's language of the 'strong contrast' between them.

---

[184] Ibid., 35.
[185] Knox, *Works*, II.279, 287.

In his discussion of Jesus' reference to his death as his baptism, Knox is right to point out the metaphorical nature of this usage. Furthermore, he is correct in saying that Christians share that baptism inasmuch as they are united with Christ on the cross.[186] It is this metaphorical link that Paul draws into his discussion of the implications of our union with Christ and its relation to baptism in Colossians 2 and Romans 6. In Colossians 2:12 Paul links baptism to union with Christ in his death. Knox took this verse to refer to Christ's baptism (i.e. his death) and stated 'there is no reference to water baptism' in the verse.[187] His reason for this is the Greek definite article before baptism which he takes to be a personal pronoun. This is a very original interpretation of this clause and does not fit particularly well with the Greek syntax. In Douglas Moo's Pillar New Testament Commentary he concludes his technical analysis of this phrase saying 'The reference is certainly to water baptism.'[188] Likewise, in his discussion of Romans 6, Knox claimed that whether Paul is referring to water baptism or Christ's 'metaphoric' baptism of death is immaterial to his argument. Nevertheless, he goes on to say 'it is highly probably [sic] that in view of Mark 10:39 the reference here to our sharing Christ's baptism is entirely metaphorical'.[189] It is worth contending that for any theology of baptism this passage's reference is hardly immaterial. Indeed, the natural reading would imply that the fact that Paul is referring to 'all of us who were baptised into Christ Jesus' (Rom 6:3) would imply water baptism is in view. Douglas Moo gives several good reasons for his conclusion about this phrase: 'Paul's reference is to the Roman Christians' water baptism...'[190]

Despite his reading of various Pauline uses of baptism as metaphorical rather than literal water baptism, Knox still maintained, 'In New Testament times, converts were baptized on their repentance in acknowledging Jesus of Nazareth as Lord (Acts 2:38, 16:31, 33). They then

---

[186] Ibid., II.293.

[187] Ibid., II.294–295.

[188] Douglas J. Moo, *The Letters to the Colossians and to Philemon*, ed. D.A. Carson, The Pillar New Testament Commentary (Grand Rapids: Eerdmans, 2008). 202.

[189] Knox, *Works*, II.295.

[190] Douglas J. Moo, *The Epistle to the Romans*, ed. Gordon Fee, The New International Commentary on the New Testament (Grand Rapids: Eerdmans, 1996). 202.

received instruction in the fundamental doctrines of the faith (Acts 2:42, Heb 6:1, 2).'[191] Nevertheless, he believed that when Paul spoke of 'one Lord, one faith, one baptism' (Eph 4:5) he was *not* referring to water baptism.[192] He bases this conclusion on his previous arguments that Paul played down the importance of water baptism in 1 Corinthians and thus, in using this word, water baptism would not have been 'uppermost in the mind of the inspired apostle.'[193] On the contrary, Knox preferred to understand Paul's use of baptism as the metaphorical use that Jesus employed to refer to his own death (Luke 12:50, Mark 10:39). The exegetical evidence for drawing this conclusion from Paul's use of the word baptism is lacking. In Leon Morris's commentary he maintained that, while it might be possible to argue about whether the apostle is primarily speaking about water baptism or baptism in the Spirit in this verse, 'surely Paul is not making such distinctions at this point'.[194] For the New Testament believer the two aspects of baptism were linked together. What is not contemplated is a metaphorical use of the term once employed by Jesus to refer to his own death, yet Knox maintained 'the inspired apostle would certainly think first of this significance when he used the word 'baptism'.'[195]

Marcia Cameron has claimed that Knox's scriptural conclusions in *New Testament Baptism* are 'highly significant' and 'all thoroughly Reformed'.[196] On the contrary, as has been demonstrated, at several points his exegesis was dubious and his conclusions alienated him from traditional Reformed theology. Indeed, in the work itself, Knox's distinct exegesis led him to disparage the history of Christian theology of baptism. He stated that the earliest Christian authors had 'a very inadequate apprehension of what the inspired authors of holy scripture were teaching'.[197] As a result, he believed water baptism came to have a place in the early church which it did not have in the New Testament and this

---

[191] Knox, *Works*, II.301.

[192] Ibid., II.302.

[193] Ibid.

[194] Leon Morris, *Expository Reflections on the Letter to the Ephesians* (Grand Rapids: Baker Books, 1994). 119.

[195] Knox, *Works*, II.303.

[196] Cameron, *Enigmatic Life*, 223.

[197] Knox, *Works*, II.304.

error had continued through history until the present.[198] In other words, Knox was not looking to be 'thoroughly Reformed' in relation to his understanding of baptism articulated in this work. The Reformers had misunderstood the Bible's teaching along with the rest of the church through the ages.

Nevertheless, despite his critique of the Christian tradition's theological rationale for water baptism, Knox maintained that 'water baptism was and is a suitable symbol for a convert to show his repentance as he accepts for the first time the imminence of the judgement day'.[199] But for those who live in a culture that has been Christianised, the biblical significance of water baptism 'is suitable for only a very few persons'.[200] In terms of reflecting this meaning, Knox made the bold claim that 'none of the interpretations of the Christian denominations have got it right'.[201] The best that can be said is that *The Book of Common Prayer* shifts the significance of water baptism the least from its New Testament significance.[202] He believed the Anglican service is essentially a service of public prayer for the child and the culmination is 'the washing of the child with water, which, in the service, is a sign, not only that the child is seen to need God's spiritual washing, but that God is a God who hears prayer and washes the child from its sins and incorporates him into Christ's body.'[203] While this means that, according to Knox, the baptism does not correspond to the meaning of the sign that was used in the New Testament, nevertheless it is a sign 'of our faith that God gives repentance (all repentance is his gift) and faith (this, too, is God's gift), in answer to prayer'.[204]

Knox concludes his treatment of New Testament baptism with this allowance: 'Water baptism was an apostolic custom and there is no reason that those who wish to continue it should not do so, so long as they do not impose on the rite a meaning inimical to the gospel.'[205] In other words, there is no imperative for Christians to administer water baptism

---

[198] Ibid.
[199] Ibid.
[200] Ibid., II.305.
[201] Ibid.
[202] Ibid., II.306.
[203] Ibid.
[204] Ibid., II.309.
[205] Ibid.

according to the Bible. If, however, some Christians choose to baptise with water they should not make baptism represent something contrary to the gospel. This can hardly be considered an endorsement for the practice and, as we have seen, it is somewhat at odds with his earlier published statements about the importance of the sacraments. In *The Thirty-Nine Articles* Knox argued that sacraments 'enable the believer to signify his response to the promises [of God] by his actions and not merely by his mental attitude or words. For example, he looks 'to God for a clear conscience' (1 Pet 3:21) as he engages in the sacramental expression of this in baptism.'[206] Likewise, in 'Justification by Faith' he said that the sacraments (both of them), are expressions of faith, and 'may properly be said to save, and are so spoken of in the New Testament.'[207] The conclusion from his unpublished *New Testament Baptism* has a somewhat different emphasis.

Weighing Up Knox's Teaching: Was He Anti-sacraments?

The issue before us then is how to weigh this unpublished source, *New Testament Baptism*, in our assessment of Knox's view of the sacraments. In this work, he rejects the traditional Christian theology of baptism, yet in other published positions he upheld and validated the classical Reformed position. Which most accurately represents his position? A generous stance would allow us to surmise that submission for publication and peer reviewed critique may have changed the final product of *New Testament Baptism* significantly. We must remember that this work was never published by Knox and it did not appear in print until the Matthias Media volume was published a decade after his death. Marcia Cameron implies that this work had the result that 'some of Broughton's disciples might well have concluded that the ceremony was unimportant'.[208] Such a conclusion based on a work that was not published until many years after Knox's death may be anachronistic. But then again, D.A. Carson recalls in Section Three of this volume that his first interaction with Knox at Tyndale House in 1982 was the Australian, having found out Carson was a Baptist, asserting that there was no water baptism in the New Testament.[209] Furthermore, Cameron records

---

[206] Knox, *Thirty-Nine Articles (1st ed.)*.
[207] Knox, *Justification by Faith*, 18.
[208] Cameron, *Enigmatic Life*, 223–224.
[209] *Legacy of Broughton Knox*, 93

elsewhere in her biography an interaction with John Newby, a lecturer at George Whitefield College, where Knox's position on baptism was a bone of contention.[210] It does seem like Knox's view on baptism was deeply held and he was prepared to defend it. The other published positions on the sacraments were written many years earlier, so perhaps we can posit that this was the position that Knox moved towards in the later years of his life.

Let us conclude by drawing together some of the threads of our evaluation. We saw early on that Knox's published sources where he deals with the topic of sacraments present a fairly consistent position that is in line with a Reformed Anglican understanding of sacraments. They are signs and seals, visible words that fortify faith in the life of the believer. We then moved on to focus on the Lord's Supper and we noted Knox's emphasis on the activity of fellowship as an end in itself. This fellowship is founded upon the word of the gospel inherent in the sacrament. Again, it is difficult to make a case that his position is anti-sacramental. Finally, we observed his thinking about baptism which certainly contained some ambiguity and idiosyncrasy. But even here, despite his conclusions about the New Testament theology of baptism, he still affirmed the Anglican rite as the most appropriate. In doing so, it is hard to justify a conclusion that he was anti-sacraments. We would be on surer ground concluding that his theological rationale for the sacraments was non-traditional, and became more so over the years, but that he maintained an important place for the sacraments in the life of the church.

A much more difficult question to answer is whether Knox's teaching has led others to an anti-sacramental position? I understand that some Anglican churches in Sydney which haven't celebrated communion for many years or don't believe in baptism often claim to be the true heirs of Knox's teaching.[211] This chapter, however, has shown that Knox did not denigrate the sacramental life of the church and as such, one wonders how he would have responded to these radical heirs.

---

[210] Cameron, *Enigmatic Life*, 311.

[211] How widespread this position is obviously is difficult to determine and is beyond the scope of this chapter, but I would guess that there are only a small minority who take things this far.

AN APPRECIATION OF D.B. KNOX'S *THE EVERLASTING GOD*

Robert Doyle

The five chapters of Broughton Knox's The *Everlasting God* were first given as the Annual Moore College Lectures of 1979, and published by Evangelical Press in 1982. They were republished by Lancer Books in 1988, and then by Matthias Media in volume 1 of *D. Broughton Knox Selected Works* in 2000, and from 2009 have remained in print as a monograph by the same company, and in e-book form. Not without reason, it is described as a 'classic work of theology ... [which] has helped many Christians to carefully examine the profoundly important subject of the character of God.'[212]

In summary, there are 5 chapters:

1.   The true and living God

2.   God of infinite power, wisdom and goodness

3.   God in Trinity

4.   One Lord Jesus Christ

5.   God who is rich in mercy (from Article 17 of 39 Articles) - i.e. predestination

As the following exposition will show, three main, related terms characterise these chapters, and indeed, Broughton's work at large: God is *personal*, God is *other-person-centred*, and *relationship*.

Each chapter follows the logic inherent in understanding the character of God, and the theme is developed progressively. The foundation is laid in chapter 1. God, in his self-revelation through the history of Israel and his incarnate Word, and then his living enscriptured Word, shows himself as personal, the true and living God, who acts in the context of a rebellious, sinful and ignorant human race to form a deeply

---

[212] Matthias Media description. URL: http://www.matthiasmedia.com.au/the-everlasting-god-ebook.

personal relationship with us, to be his sons and daughters, that is, like Abraham, his friends. Chapter 2 would in the standard terminology of classical theism be titled the attributes of God. Three attributes of the living and true God are identified and developed following the trajectory of creation, our sinful condition, judgement, the cross and salvation. The three are infinite power, wisdom and goodness. And again, they are understood not in the context of a definition of God as an 'infinite substance', but in the context of God as person, having personal action that implies purpose, which implies assessment, responsibility and authority. Chapter 3 then examines God as he is apically revealed in the Father's sending of the incarnate Son and the Spirit, God in Trinity. Again, the main leitmotif is carried in the emphasis on the doctrine of the Trinity revealing that reality involves relationships. Along with the scriptural presentation, articulating the one undivided nature and actions of God in his tri-personal particularity, and identifying the primacy of the Father in these relations, considerable attention is given to the person and work of the Spirit, and thus our re-creation in the image of God. Chapter 4 returns to a closer examination of our One Lord Jesus Christ, in his self-testimony and the path of his saving actions on our behalf which will culminate in his final parousia. Chapter 5, in an exploration of predestination, brings together the heavenly and eternal reality and purposes of God with their earthly outworking. For, somewhat against common apprehension, it is here in its teaching on predestination that the Scriptures most acutely identify God as 'the God who is rich in mercy' (Eph. 1:4-12, 2:4). The basic Christian concept of God is that he is gracious. God then, the living and true God, who in his triune relations is Father, Son and Spirit, in his infinite power, wisdom and goodness has in mercy and love acted sovereignly to save us. That is our comfort, and motive power for ethical living.

Having outlined the contents, I will seek to expose some of riches of Broughton's book under three headings: heuristic method, some bold moves, and assessment against contemporary scholarship.

Heuristic Method

Each chapter is persistently existential because the nature of reality is that the living and merciful triune God of Holy Scripture has made a creation other than himself to dwell beside him in fellowship and dependence on him. Broughton's accurate and often acute observations of the human condition and the scriptural data about the character and actions of the living God form a heuristic vehicle that catches up the reader or listener into God's saving works. It fosters both self-recognition in the light of the knowledge of God being unfolded, and faith in him and his saving work. This movement is anchored at the divine end by the character of God, both in his own being and his actions towards us, as other-person-centred. And at the human end, anchored by the fact that being created in his image, we are created for relationship.

Chapter 1 is typical. We begin with being told that the concept of God is innate, and readily understood, not that the idea is fully formed in our minds, but that as soon as we are told about it, we accept it. 'Religion and belief in the divine are co-extensive with humanity.'[213] Closer analysis follows: 'Strictly speaking, it is responsiveness to the concept of deity which is innate.' Further,

> The ingredients that make up this universally held concept include personality and everlastingness, as well as knowledge, power and relatedness. The deities, as humanity conceives of them, are eternal, superhuman beings who influence our lives, and who in turn may be influenced by a right approach to them.

What follows is a careful analysis into its component elements of the main concern of the chapter, that deity is quintessentially personal and thus self-revelational. So we move into, and for his students this is familiar territory, three recurring foundational ideas: persons are self-authenticating, God is known in his Word, and the testimony of Jesus and of the New Testament prophets and apostles is that the Christian Bible is the enscriptured living word of God. Congruent notes follow on the infallible and inerrant nature of Scripture, which, as it reaches our ears as God's own word, forms a response in us that brings knowledge and trust and thus fellowship.

There are several things to note. First, the opening appeal to ordinary human experience is not an apologetic in the sense that an external foundation of reasonableness has been found in human experience, that is, this is not a 'natural theology'. It is the strategy Paul uses in Athens at the Areopagus, where he directs his hearers to their own poets for a statement of the truth that 'in him we live and move and have

---

[213] D.B. Knox, 'The Everlasting God' in Knox, *Works*, I.38.

our being' (Acts 17:28). Paul has already established the truth by announcing it from Holy Scripture: that the world is the creation of God and dependent on him and that in the face of impending judgment, to be executed by the resurrected Jesus Christ, we ought repent, flee idolatry and cling only to this God. The facts of the case come from God's self-revelation, and close observation of human existence discovers and points to a resonant expression in an innate knowledge of our existence and dependence on deity. Further, as the narrative of Acts indicates, and Broughton's last chapter brings to the fore, this gospel arrives and takes root not on a foundation agreed on by a universal common sense, but, even despite the latter, creates its own landing ground in the hard hearts of its hearers, for as at Antioch in Pisidia, 'as many as were ordained to eternal life believed (Acts 13:48).'

Broughton's placing of ordinary human and Christian experience as a first step in his heuristic strategy comes, then, because the Bible explicitly or implicitly has done that. That is, the Bible speaks to us of where we are. Nor is the identification forced. On the contrary, in chapter 5 on predestination Broughton points out that we can only explore its meaning and consequences from within revelation itself, because 'the relationship of the supreme will of Almighty God and the subordinate but real wills of men and women is a difficult one, . . there is no parallel in our experience to help us understand it.'[214] That is, with respect to method, throughout Broughton does theology *a posteriori*, after the fact.

Second, and as already indicated, he argues primarily from Scripture, its narrative from creation to new creation, the biblical theology progressively developed from Old to New Testaments, the theological themes and the concrete propositional data of the texts. Approaching the Bible in this way naturally means that his use is more inductive than deductive, although once a foundational truth is established, deduction is used to indicate the consequences. For example, on the description of the attributes of God in Article 1 of the 39 Articles of Faith, that God is 'without parts', Broughton states:

> 'Without parts' is inherent in the concept of spirit. God is spirit and spirit is not composite, made up of parts as material objects are. Spirit is not divisible, Jesus taught

---

[214] Ibid., I.125.

that God is spirit. Our knowledge of spirit comes from our knowledge of ourselves. We know that we are an indivisible unity.[215]

An example of how his scripturally orientated heuristic method works can be seen in the christological focus Broughton uses to explain the divine attribute of wisdom:

> God is of infinite wisdom. Wisdom may be defined as knowledge applied in purposeful activity to achieve good ends. Knowledge applied purposefully but not towards the good of others is not called wisdom but cunning. Wisdom must always be good. Wickedness is incompatible with wisdom... God's wisdom is marvellously displayed in the created world. As the psalmist exclaims, 'O Yahweh, how many are your works! In wisdom you have made them all.' [Ps.104:24] The world has been created to accomplish ends of blessing, of joy and of fellowship with God. It marvellously achieves these ends. Take for example our body ... the body is marvellously contrived to accomplish its ends of relationship, with all the pleasure, physical, mental, emotional, spiritual that relationship brings... Our sexual natures, both psychological and physical, are marvellously designed to relate us in joyous fellowship.
>
> God's wisdom is manifest in creation but is even more marvellously displayed in redemption and the restoration of fellowship with God. God has bestowed upon us every spiritual blessing. These blessings are in Jesus Christ. He is the wisdom of God. He is so described by Paul in 1 Corinthians 1:24. God's beneficence comes to fruition in Christ and in his cross. Paul expresses this in Colossians 2:3 - 'Christ, in whom are all the treasures of wisdom ... hidden'.[216]

Then follows two pages unpacking the redemptive fruits that come from Christ, the Wisdom of God.

---

[215] Ibid., I.63.
[216] Ibid., I.68–70.

Third, as already apparent, Broughton's analysis is marked by accurate and acute observation, which greatly assists its existential, pastoral impact, better fostering our relationship together with God. Logical and insightful criticism of contemporary thought and social practice, both within and outside the church, abound. So, in the face of the universal, innate presence of the concept of deity, and that deity is personal, as witnessed 'in religion as a universal activity', Broughton observes 'the acceptance of [deity's] non-existence can only be maintained by constant propaganda'.[217] To which we might now add, and censorship! Similarly, the foolish and self-damning idolatry of our use of evolution theory is exposed:

> All the beauty and intricacy and all the marvellous arrangements of the natural world are supposed to have been evolved by a thoughtless, purposeless, mechanical operation of nature, and in this way the God who made the world is as effectively shut out of the minds of those who are enjoying the blessings of his creations as he was by the false religions of idolatry. Just as the idolaters could not see the foolishness, indeed the stupidity, of worshipping gods of wood and stone, which have no life nor purpose nor mind, so modern believers in the theory of evolution cannot see the foolishness of that theory...[218]

And a final example of acute observation, which cuts to the heart of the Christian churches, on the gospel of judgment:

> A gospel which contains judgement as a prominent strand, as does the New Testament gospel, is relevant to men and women everywhere and in very age and culture. It does not need indigenization [i.e. contextualisation], so popular a catchword today, but requires only clarity of language and faithfulness in proclamation. The sense of right and wrong is universal in the human race ... [and then attention is turned to contemporary preaching] A gospel that minimizes or omits judgement must concentrate on this life and the benefits that Christ brings for this life. Most modern preaching, whether liberal or

---

[217] Ibid., I.38–39.
[218] Ibid., I.55.

evangelical, falls into this mistake... But the Christian gospel is concerned with the future. It proclaims Jesus who rescues us from the wrath to come. [1 Thess. 1:10]. When hearers accept the gospel for the benefits of this life, such as peace and happiness, it is a contradiction to ask them to suffer for the gospel...[219]

And so on.

Some Bold Exegetical Moves

Both his work in the classroom and publications show that, convinced by adequate evidence and argument, Broughton's work with the text of Scripture was characterised by bold exegetical moves that had the potential to yield far reaching theological consequences.

Pistis Christou is the Faith/Faithfulness of Jesus Christ

In passing, a well-known move, which was important to his understanding of Jesus' work primarily in terms of obedience, was taking *pistis Christou* in Romans 3:22, Galatians 3:22, and Philippians 3:9 as the subjective genitive, 'the faith/faithfulness of Christ.'[220] Further, having made that move, he then applied it to the enigmatic, 'the righteousness of God *from faith to faith*' of Romans 1:17, to give it a christological solution: 'the meaning becomes crystal clear when it is seen that the first reference is to Jesus' faith and the second reference is to the faith which we in response exercise towards him.'[221] At least concomitant, and certainly earlier in time, is the short essay in 1970 of Broughton's colleague, Donald Robinson, "Faith of Jesus Christ - a New Testament debate.'[222] The reading of *pistis Christou* as a subjective genitive continued at Moore College with Peter O'Brien.[223] Although it has not

---

[219] Ibid., I.60–61.

[220] Ibid., I.111.

[221] Ibid., I.112.

[222] Andrew M. Leslie, "Christ's Faithfulness and Our Salvation," in *Donald Robinson Selected Works: Appreciation*, ed. Peter Bolt (Camperdown N.S.W.: Australian Church Record/Moore College, 2008), 73.

[223] Peter O'Brien, *The Epistle to the Philippians: A Commentary on the Greek Text* (Grand Rapids: Eerdmans, 1991). 396, 398–400.

met with universal approval, nevertheless, the case for it is considerable.[224]

But, I want to highlight two other exegetical moves which are arguably bolder, and given that they are well founded, also yield far reaching theological consequences.

God's Maintaining of His Prior Covenant with Creation – Genesis 9:9-10

In exploring the attributes of God, in chapter 2 Broughton argues that 'goodness in relationship involves responsibility.'

> The act of creation brings the Creator into a relationship of responsibility for the welfare of his creation. For otherwise God would not be good. From the moment of creation, the good God is in a relationship of care and concern for that which he brought into being, and his care and concern are infinite and never vary or fail.[225]

To strengthen the point he then states, 'we may say that God is in a covenant relationship with his creation from the inceptions of its existence. In the true world were goodness is basic, creation involves covenant', and so on.

Now, the idea of a primal covenant is not new in Reformed thought, which has since Dudley Fenner (c. 1558–87) posited a 'covenant of works' between God and Adam pre-Fall. But, in line with John Murray's observation in 1954 that the basis of all God's covenants with men is grace and promise,[226] Broughton states 'the covenant is always a

---

[224] Ibid. Also, the case for an objective genitive, refer James Dunn, "Once More PISTIS CHRISTOU," in *Pauline Theology*, ed. E.E. Johnson and D.M. Hay (Atlanta: Scholars Press, 1997), IV.61–68. And for both objective and subjective, S.K. Williams, "Again πιστις Χριστου," *Catholic Biblical Quarterly* 49 (1987): 431–447.

[225] Knox, *Works*, I.64.

[226] John Murray's seminal paper on covenant concludes: 'This brings to a close our review of the evidence bearing upon the nature of God's covenant with men. From the beginning of God's disclosures to men in terms of covenant we find a unity of conception which is to the effect that a divine covenant is a sovereign administration of grace and of promise. It is not compact or contract or agreement that provides the constitutive or governing idea but that of

An Appreciation of D.B. Knox's *The Everlasting God*

covenant of grace'. Further, 'Its character and content will vary with humanity's situation and need.'[227] Thus far, then, Broughton has arrived at his conclusion by on the one hand an induction from the broad biblical narrative about God's dealings with his creation, his *rebellious* creation, which is marked by many covenantal ceremonies and promises, and on the other, a deduction from the nature of the asymmetrical relationship which exists between persons, between God and humankind.

Then follows the bold exegetical assertion: 'The covenant, implicit in creation, becomes explicit in Genesis 6 and 9. In these passages, God promises that he will maintain his covenant. "I will *maintain* my covenant with you and with your seed after you and with every living creature that is with you."' The only footnote seeming to justify this translation is to the Revised Version, Genesis 9:9-10, which of course, has not 'maintain' but 'establish'! Where may have this come from? Broughton's colleague, Bill Dumbrell, does not publish his *Creation and Covenant* until 1984. Here he advances linguistic and contextual arguments for taking הקים hēqîm [hiphil of קום qūm] as not 'establish' (usually כות kārat 'to cut'), but 'confirm'. We may perhaps infer a Faculty common room discussion. Or, has there been influence from the earlier arguments by Karl Barth in his Kirchliche Dogmatik volumes III.1 and IV.1 of 1945 and 1953 (English translations 1958 and 1956 respectively) for the covenant with Noah expressing the prior covenant by Yahweh with his creation? On Genesis 9:9-10, Barth's argument is not linguistic, but like Broughton's, contextual, with close attention paid to the fact that the covenant with

---

dispensation in the sense of disposition. This central and basic concept is applied, however, to a variety of situations and the precise character of the grace bestowed and of the promise given differs in the differing covenant administrations. The differentiation does not reside in any deviation from this basic conception but simply consists in the differing degrees of richness and fullness of the grace bestowed and of the promise given. Preponderantly in the usage of Scripture covenant refers to grace and promise specifically redemptive. The successive covenants are coeval with the successive epochs in the unfolding and accomplishment of God's redemptive will.' *Covenant of Grace* (London: Tyndale Press, 1954); refer http://www.the-highway.com/Covenant_Murray.html. See also his keen historical and systematic survey of the notions of covenant in the Reformed tradition, John Murray, "Covenant Theology," in *Collected Writings of John Murray: Volume Four* (Edinburgh: Banner of Truth Trust, 1982), 216–240.

[227] Knox, *Works*, I.64.

Noah explicitly includes 'every living creature that is with you, the birds, the cattle, and every beast of the earth with you; of all that go out of the ark, even every beast of the earth.' That is, we are taken back to Genesis 1 and 2.

By way of assessment, we note that despite scholarly criticism in the field of biblical studies, Bill's arguments continue to persuade.[228] And Bill himself recently, in work published in 2007 and 2013, has engaged with the arguments by Paul Williamson that contest against a covenant with creation.[229]

To my mind, Barth's and Knox's contextual, biblical theological, arguments are strong. The living and true God, who as an act of grace has created something other than himself, but in his image, to live beside him in fellowship, has in that act and the following cycle of judgment and grace in Genesis 3-12, pledged himself to his creation for its continued good, which is restoration of relation to himself. The Hebrew of Genesis 9:9 will allow both 'maintain' and 'establish'. Context pushes us towards 'maintain', and that underscores God's deep personal commitment to us, in the face of our sin and ignorance. The benefits of this exegetical move follow. Barth perceptively observes the intertwined relation of grace between Creator and creatures, 'Creation is the outward basis of the covenant (Gen. 1) and the covenant the inward basis of creation (Gen. 2).'[230] Broughton articulates its consequences from the foundation of the doctrine of God:

> God's covenant relationship with creation, when expressed in personal terms, means that he is faithful: he fulfils that which he promises. He is the faithful God and we are to reflect his faithfulness in our relationships, not

---

[228] E.g. recently P.J. Gentry and S.J. Wellum, *God's Kingdom through God's Covenants* (Wheaton: Crossway, 2015). 65, cf 59–61. And earlier Gordon J. Wenham, *Genesis 1-15* (Waco, TX: Word Books, 1987). 175.

[229] William J. Dumbrell, "A Covenant with Creation (Genesis 6:18) and Jesus and the New Covenant (Luke 22:20)," *Reformed Theological Review* Supplement Series 2(2007): 148ff. And William J. Dumbrell, *Covenant and Creation: An Old Testament Covenant Theology*, 2nd ed. (Milton Keynes: Paternoster, 2013). 8–20.

[230] Karl Barth, *Church Dogmatics* (Edinburgh: T&T Clarke, 1974). IV.1.27 (also III.21.41).

only with God, but with one another... . The faithfulness of God is the most important aspect of his goodness. Without this divine attribute of faithfulness it would not be possible to practice the Christian religion, because the Christian religion is a relationship which calls for the response of obedience and hope.[231]

John 17:5 'the glory', which Jesus Prays the Father to be Restored to, is the Holy Spirit

Finally, and without any precedent that I can find, Broughton argued that 'the glory' which Jesus prays to be restored to in John 17:5 is the Holy Spirit. And, it is noted, there is no explicit reference at all in this chapter to the Spirit.

> The Spirit is the glory, that is, the manifestation of the character of God. Christ prays for his return to the previous relationship of glory which he had with the Father from eternity. 'Glorify me together with yourself, Father, with the glory which I had with you before the world was.'

The surrounding sentences are short, containing many concepts following one on another, without much in the way of extended or direct reference to the text of John nor exposition. But, his justification of this exegetical conclusion moves on two fronts.

First, Broughton invokes God's triune nature and the divinity of Jesus as portrayed in John's Gospel. 'Absolute equality between the Father and the Son in the divine attributes is clearly enunciated.' Jesus has everything from the Father, including divine glory. 'The Father is related to the Son, and the Son to the Father, through the Holy Spirit.' All that is supportable from John's Gospel - refer John 14: 7, 9, 10, 11; 17:21; and 1:1-5, 14, 18. With respect to the Spirit mediating the relation of the Father to the Son in the economy of salvation, we have in John and the Synoptics at the beginning of Jesus' ministry the descent of the Holy Spirit upon him at his baptism (Jn. 1:29-34). And more widely in the Synoptics and John, the Spirit is the presence and power of God at Jesus'

---

[231] Knox, *Works*, I.65.

conception (Mt. 1:18, 20; Lk. 1:35), temptation in the wilderness (Mt. 4:1; Lk. 4:1), and ministry (Lk. 4:14, 18; 10:21; Mt. 12:18, 28; Jn. 3:34).

Second, Broughton identifies the role the Spirit plays as it is more widely attested in John, and especially with respect to the triune relation of unity and love seen in the economy of salvation and Jesus dealings with the disciples. 'The Spirit is also implied in the unity arising from the mutuality of indwelling of the Father and the Son as do believers with the Father and the Son [Jn. 17:21].'

> The glory is the bond of unity between ourselves, one with another, as well as between ourselves and God. 'The glory which you have given me I have given them; *that they may be one, just as we are one, I in them and you in me* [Jn. 17:22-23].' The Spirit is the glory for the Spirit is the bond. Christ's prayer for unity of his followers with one another and with God was fulfilled at Pentecost with the gift of the Spirit. The Spirit is oneness. The Spirit is the glory. The Spirit is love. The Spirit is the bond between Father and the Son and between God and the believer, for the Spirit is the glory and the love. The Spirit's presence is the presence of Christ and the presence of love. Christ prayed, 'The love wherewith you loved me may in them, and I in them [Jn. 17:26].' [emphasis mine][232]

By way of summary evaluation, as well as the term 'glory' designating divinity in its fullness, and at John 17:5 it *is* used immanently, throughout John in the economy of salvation the Spirit is determinative for the revelatory and re-creative work of the incarnate Logos, the illumination, the bonding or communion in love, the unity, that his person and work produces – 1:33; 3:5-6; 3:34; 6:63; 7:39; 14:passim; 15:26; 16:12-15; 20:19-22. Thus the Spirit *is* implied in 17:5, 21, 22-23a, 23-25, 26. That is, Broughton's intuition that Holy Spirit is 'implied' is well founded. As expected, his application of that exegetical insight is to the point: 'It is a grave theological mistake to think that our Lord's prayer for the unity of Christians is still to be fulfilled. It was answered at Pentecost.'[233]

---

[232] Ibid., I.81–82.
[233] Ibid., I.82.

An Assessment against Contemporary Scholarship in Systematic Theology

In this last section I want to move the focus to an assessment more from the point of view of systematic theology contemporary with us. Five points in brief.

Method in Trinitarian Thought

David Coffey, of the Catholic Institute of Sydney (formerly St Patrick's Manly), then Marquette University, in a dialogue with Scripture and the Church Fathers (especially Augustine), and Karl Rahner, has written extensively and influentially on the doctrine of the Trinity. One of his points of contention is that today a common methodological assumption is that we move from the data of the Bible, the 'biblical doctrine of the Trinity', to the economic Trinity, and only then the immanent Trinity. 'I would be critical of this. I see the economic Trinity as the last step of the argument, the integration of the biblical data with the knowledge of the immanent Trinity that has been extrapolated from them.' That is, Coffey argues, the more accurate method, and that of Augustine and the other Fathers, is the movement of our minds from the 'biblical Trinity' as the earthly sign or revelation, directly to discerning the immanent Trinity from these revelatory signs, with delineation of the economic Trinity as the last step in a process of integration of the biblical presentation with what we learn there of God in himself.[234] Or, as John reports Jesus, 'He who has seen me has seen the Father (Jn. 14:9).' Here, we may situate Broughton.

In Augustine, Uncharacteristically, the Holy Spirit as the Mutual Love of the Father and the Son is Not Argued from Scripture

Second, in accord with the evidence, Coffey points out that *un*characteristically in his advancing of his distinctive mutual love theory - that the Holy Spirit is the mutual love of the Father and the Son, their common bond - Augustine does *not* move from the text of Scripture. For

---

[234] 'It is from these data that the doctrine of the immanent Trinity is inferred by the Church over a period of four centuries, and along with it, by an automatic process of integration, the doctrine of the economic Trinity as the conclusion of this illative process.' David Coffey, "The Holy Spirit as the Mutual Love of the Father and the Son," *Theological Studies* 51(1990): 194–195.

Augustine, the Holy Spirit as the mutual love between the Father and the Son is a deduction from the *filioque* (he proceeds from the Father and the Son) which Augustine points out is the direct attestation of John's Gospel (Jn. 14:26; 15:26; 20:22). Part of the work Coffey does is to mount a more explicit biblical argument for the mutual love theory from the gospel narratives and the epistles. One of his observations is that in the New Testament the Holy Spirit is very often associated with the concept of Christian love - e.g. Galatians 5:16, 22; Romans 5:5. In his compressed style, I have sought to ague, Broughton has done the same. As a footnote, David Coffey's work on pneumatology, and then of Thomas Weinandy and more recently near us in New Zealand, Myk Habets, has produced what is termed 'Third Article Theology', which shows much promise in further illuminating our understanding of the Trinity. Ah, if only Broughton was here to enjoy the pursuit, and bring his critical mind to bear.

The Priority of the Father

Third, although only lightly, but carefully stated in *Everlasting God*, and at more length in Appendix B of the St Matthias edition,[235] Broughton has been much criticised for the priority he gives to the Father in the order of the inner triune relations, an order he argues the Bible applies to human relationships, and most contentiously, between men and women. It is not disputed that there is a strong Father-centred order in the economy of salvation. But many, including T.F. Torrance, while recognising there is an immanent order, for the Son is eternally begotten of the Father, and the Spirit proceeds from the Father and thus the Son, nevertheless feel the need to close down the question of the priority of the Father. Torrance is driven by what he fears is an inchoate ontological subordinationism of an Arian kind lying in the Cappadocian Fathers description of this order in terms of the Father being the 'cause' of the Son and the Spirit. In the wider, more popular debate, especially amongst Evangelicals, the Catholic theologian Steven Boyer has observed that in the last two centuries there has been 'dramatic changes in the social context of the Western world, and many Christian theologians today work in a culture in which equality is the dominant principle. Hence, the equality of the divine Persons is easily granted in contemporary discussion, whereas the notion of order in the Trinity is often addressed with less conviction, and sometimes even

---

[235] Ibid., 153–170.

with suspicion.' By contrast, the Church Fathers, and Boyer takes Athanasius as a key example, were comfortable in affirming equality *and order* within the Godhead.[236] A consequence of Torrance's studied reticence is that although he has much to say about the identity of the Son and the Spirit, he has less to say about the Father's particularity. In his magisterial *The Trinitarian Faith* (1988) and *The Christian Doctrine of God* (1996), he pays only slight attention to the eternal generation of the Son and scant deliberation regarding the Father as the *first* Person.

What is happening in some contemporary research and scholarship is a re-engagement with the Fathers, and the later tradition that followed them into the early 18th century. There is good evidence emerging that these theologians, along with equality of the persons, affirmed the priority of the Father in the divine processions, in their mutual or perichoretic relations, and the divine attributes, especially authority.

By way of example, take Augustine. According to Augustine, the Father is 'the one principle from whom all things come',[237] and, 'only the Father is called the one from whom the Word is born and from whom the Holy Spirit principally proceeds'.[238] He puts the Father's ontological primacy in these terms:

> it is clear that the Son has another from whom he is and whose Son he is, while the Father does not have a Son from whom he is, but only whose Father he is. Every son gets being what he is from his father, and is his father's son; while no father gets what he is from his son, though he is his son's father.[239]

---

[236] Steven D. Boyer, "Articulating Order: Trinitarian Discourse in an Egalitarian Age," *Pro Ecclesia* 18, no. 3 (2009): 255–256.

[237] Augustine, *Epistula XI.4* (CCSL 31: 28.88–99); The Works of St Augustine II/1. Letters. Vol. 1 No. 1-99, trans. Roland J Teske, ed., Boniface Ramsey (Hyde Park, NY: New City Press, 2001) 37.

[238] Augustine, *De Trinitate*, XV.29; tr. Hill, 419.

[239] Augustine, *De Trinitate*, II.2; tr. Hill, 98.

He describes the Son's power in this way:

> the Son's power is from the Father, that is why the Son's substance too is from the Father; and because the Son's substance is from the Father, that is why the Son's power too is from the Father. And so, because the Son is from the Father, that is why he said, *The Son can do nothing of his own.* Because the Son does not get 'is' from himself, that is why he does not get 'can' from himself either.[240]

And Augustine stresses, that is why the person and power of the Son, although from the Father, is not less than that of the Father. The Son 'was not sent in virtue of some disparity of power or substance or anything in him that was not equal to the Father, but in virtue of the Son being from the Father, not the Father being from the Son.'[241]

In his remarks on the fundamentally relational Being of God, employing the term *koinōnia*, Basil of Caesarea similarly assumes the Father's unrepeatable primacy within 'the distinction of Persons ... according to the community of nature (*koinōnia*)', i.e. in their mutuality, or to use John of Damascus term, *perichoresis*. Their mutual *koinōnia*, their unity, follows from the processions, and the Father's primacy in them:

> Worshipping as we do God of God, we both confess the distinction of the Persons, and at the same time abide by the Monarchy. We do not fritter away the theology in a divided plurality, because one form, so to say, united in the invariableness of the Godhead, is beheld in God the Father, and in God the only begotten. For the Son is in the Father and the Father in the Son; since such as is the latter, such is the former, and such as is the former, such is the latter; and herein is the unity. So that according to the distinction of Persons, both are one and one, and

---

[240] Augustine, *Homilies on the Gospel of John* 1-40, 20.4; The Works of Saint Augustine I/12, trans., Edmund Hill, ed., Allan Fitzgerald (Hyde Park, NY: New City Press, 2009), 361.

[241] Augustine, *De Trinitate*, IV.27; tr. Hill, 172.

according to the community of Nature, one (kata de *to koinon tēs phuseōs, hen hoi amphoteroi.*[242]

In other words, according to Basil, we find the divine unity by affirming from the processions, in which the Father has the primacy, the interpersonal relation of utterly unique Persons, which is their fellowship or community of nature.

Finally, we may note there is ongoing careful work on the best systematic way to express this priority. In this context, 'Third Article Theology' argues that reciprocally in the eternal divine processions from the Father, the Son and the Spirit 'person' the Father. This rests on both the eternal begotteness of the Son and on the Spirit being the divine mutual love of the Father and the Son in the *filioque*.

Broughton's careful affirmation of the priority of the Father, then, has a growing scholarly support.

An Underdeveloped Opportunity in Understanding the Obedience of Christ: Christ's Solidarity with Us; and His Ongoing Priestly Work

Fourth, an assessment of his chapter, and other writings, with respect to the person and work of Christ. In his close examination in chapter 4 of our 'One Lord Jesus Christ', in Jesus' self-testimony that he is God and his acceptance on our behalf of the limitations of his real human nature, and the path of his saving actions which will culminate in his final parousia, Broughton very helpfully concentrates on the 'faith/fullness', the obedience of Jesus Christ and that he is, on behalf of the Father, Lord over earth and heaven. The perceptive pastoral consequences he draws fall within this trajectory.

What is understated in this chapter, and surprisingly so in a pastorally orientated exposition of the obedience of Christ, is Christ's solidarity with us as the second Adam, the second head of the human race, and that concomitantly, Christ is our priest, who continues to pray for us at the right hand of the Father. But aspects of it are identified here and elsewhere in his writings. The descriptions may be brief, but they are, as expected, acute in their critical acumen and their focus on our restored fellowship. In stating the relation between Adam and Christ, Broughton does so by identifying the contrasts. The solidarity is, of course, assumed,

---

[242] Basil, *De Spiritu Sancto* XVIII.45; NPNF 2.8:45.

otherwise the contrasts would not work. But the focus is on the fulfilment of God's purpose for humanity in his incarnate Son, hence the contrast with Adam. That certainly follows the trajectory of the New Testament, e.g. Hebrews 2:5-9.

> The New Testament has more than one way of referring to Christ's obedience... Man's fundamental sin in the Garden of Eden was disobedience ... Christ reversed that disobedience, being the first man ever perfectly to obey the will of our heavenly Father and to obey it in every conceivable manner of testing... the contrast between Adam's disobedience and Christ's obedience is very clear in Romans 5 ...[243]

And his acceptance of the Reformation mainstream's understanding of the human nature Jesus assumed, fallen or unfallen, is in line with this:

> When the Son of God became man, it was man's nature in its pristine goodness that he took, not the defective self-centred, rebellious nature we inherit as the entail of Adam's sin. He did not partake of the sin of independence from God, or of independent knowledge, which was forbidden man at his creation.[244]

Yet:

> His faith was tested in a way that ours never will be. God asked of him a form of obedience which he never will ask

---

[243] Ibid., 107.

[244] 'Jesus' knowledge', in Knox, *Works*, I.236. For a statement and defence of the alternative view, assumption of fallen nature, and its positive entailments expressed as 'the great exchange', refer T. F. Torrance, *Incarnation: The Person and Life of Christ* (Milton Keynes: Paternoster, 2008). 61–67. And T.F. Torrance, *The Trinitarian Faith* (Edinburgh: T&T Clark, 1993). 179–190. E.g. 'He incorporated the ignorance of men in himself, that he might redeem their humanity from all its imperfections and cleanse and offer it perfect and holy to the Father [186].' For interaction with the contemporary debate and further explication, see E. Mwale, "A Theological Evaluation of T.F. Torrance's Understanding of the Humanity of Christ: The Free Divine Movement as a Paradigm for Understanding the Incarnational Vicarious Assumption of a Fallen Human Nature" (unpublished MTh dissertation, North-West University, 2016).

AN APPRECIATION OF D.B. KNOX'S *THE EVERLASTING GOD*

of us. God asked that he, the perfect man, should identify himself so completely with sinful man that he became sin for us and experienced all that sin involves.[245]

Broughton also affirms that 'Jesus Christ is our mediator', and elucidates it in terms of his priesthood and the fellowship it brings with God:

> [T]he New Testament writers urge Christians to be aware of this great privilege that through Christ each may, himself, enter directly into God's presence. No intermediary is needed, apart from that great high priest, our saviour Jesus Christ... We live in God's presence. This is the privilege of being a child of God, which is ours through our relationship to God's only Son, Jesus Christ. Nor do we need to offer any further sacrifice than that of Jesus Christ made once for all on Calvary for us.[246]

The foundation of the Christian's fellowship with God, and each other, is that Christ is our praise leader, who intercedes for us:

> The scriptures speak of the believers' fellowship with God in several areas of activity. Of Jesus it is said: "in the midst of the church (ἐκκλησια *ekklesia*) will I sing your praise" (Heb 2:12). We are one with Christ in his leadership of praise to God in the heavenly church of which we are members. Indeed the whole of the created world joins with the redeemed in this praise of God (Rev 4:9-10, 5:5-14, 7:9-12). And of us it is said: *Teaching and admonishing yourselves with psalms and hymns and spiritual songs, singing with grace in your hearts unto God (Col 3:16)* ... Of Jesus we read, "He ever lives to make intercession for those who draw hear to God through him" (Heb 7:25) ... Of us, we are promised: "If anyone sees his brother sinning a sin not unto death he shall ask and [God] shall give him life" (1 John 5:16)... and let them pray ... (James 5:15) ... Christ prayed for us in the upper room (John 17). He prays for us now. The Spirit prays for us. The Spirit helps our intercession. We are to have

---

[245] Knox, *Works*, I.105.
[246] Knox, 'Heaven is People', in ibid., II.251.

82

AN APPRECIATION OF D.B. KNOX'S *THE EVERLASTING GOD*

fellowship with one another in our prayers.[247] [emphasis original]

And on the relation we may suppose between Adam and us, and thus Christ and us, in a note dated April 1979, he insightfully pinpoints the flaw in some Reformed expositions of the representative nature of Christ's person and work, and affirms the realism of the scriptural presentation. It is worth quoting in full:

> It took the theologians of the post-Reformation period to explain the transmission of sin in terms of the federal or covenant relationship in which Adam stood to God on behalf of the race, so that when the head of the covenant fell, he dragged the race with him. This idea is central to Covenant Theology as a whole, since its basic principle is that since man was ruined through a representative, man can be restored through a representative. [Quoting RA Findlayson, *The Story of Theology* (London: Tyndale press, 1963, p. 30] There is nothing in the Scriptures to suggest this covenant concept. Man's relationship to Adam is much more realistic than his being a nominated representative. Similarly, the Christian (who is in Christ) has a relationship to Christ that is real as can be. He was "in Christ", crucified with him, raised with him. In Covenant Theology, it is plain that Christ can only represent the elect. Hence limited atonement, presumably.[248]

By way of comparison, John Calvin not only starts with a careful examination of Christ's assumption of our humanity, and his solidarity with us in it, but configures the person and work of Christ under the leading concept of 'mediator', who discharges this function through the three offices of prophet, priest, and king.[249] In this, Calvin, and before him Athanasius, following the logic of Galatians 4:4-5, understands the relationship between the incarnate Son and the Father, and thus between us and God, primarily in terms of *filial* relationship: the Father has sent

---

[247] Knox, 'The Biblical Concept of Fellowship' in ibid., II.64–65.
[248] Ibid., I.361.
[249] John Calvin, *Institutes of the Christian Religion*, ed. John T. McNeill, trans. Ford Lewis Battles (Philadelphia: Westminster, 1960). 2.12–17.

83

forth his Son to make us his sons and daughters by adoption. Christ's obedience, of course, falls within this structure, which identifies the fuller scope of his person and work. Christ, our brother and Lord, who in his work as prophet, priest, and king, is in his person as well as his work the propitiation for our sins (1 John 2:4), continues at the right hand of the Father to pray for us. Attention to these wider, more foundational and encompassing truths offers, I would argue, even more astute pastoral insights.

If I may be permitted to reflect on this from the point of view of traditional African religion. Many African Christians wonder if it is better to return to African traditional powers to address spiritual insecurity. That is, many African Christians struggle to see how Jesus Christ relates to their terrors and fears which emanate from their traditional beliefs in spiritual powers. Is Jesus a sufficient mediator?

African traditional religion is generally characterised by two main elements.[250] First, by a spiritual structure of ultimate divinity and lesser divinities, mediating ancestors, and mediating sangomas who advise on the sacrifices necessary to appease the mediating ancestors and other spirits, and bring a good outcome. Second, the importance of community in determining who are the worthy ancestor spirits that are working in a mediatorial way in this spiritual chain. In the midst of terrors and fears which emanate from their traditional beliefs in spiritual powers, many African Christians wonder if Jesus, who is not a member of their community, and not as such approved by the community as an ancestor-mediator, is sufficient to address their spiritual insecurities.

Hebrews chapters 1 and 2 argue that Jesus is the only one who can deal with our spiritual insecurities, of whatever type they are. He alone is fully qualified to do so. He is not only truly God (chapter 1), but also our brother, our proper and new and merciful and loving and empathetic founding ancestor, who has completely healed the gap between the one true God and us, and conquered all evil and chaos. 'For

---

[250] I am indebted here to Kwame Bediako, 'Jesus in African Culture: a Ghanaian perspective' in his Kwame Bediako, *Jesus in Africa: The Christian Gospel in African History and Experience* (Cumbria: Paternoster, 2004). 20–33. And to the research of MA student, Chris Magezi, "The Conceptualization of Christ's Salvation in Kwame Bediako and Thomas F. Torrance and Its Implications for Spiritual Security in African Christianity" (unpublished MA dissertation, North West University, 2015).

he partook of the same things, our flesh and blood, that through death he might destroy the one who has the power of death, that is, the devil, and deliver all those who through fear of death were subject to lifelong slavery' (Heb. 2:14). It is this high priest who continues to uphold us in his intercessions on our behalf.

Predestination

Finally, an assessment of Broughton's examination of predestination. He accurately sets the doctrine and identifies the other doctrines within which it sits and which give rise to it, and thus control it - especially the doctrines of God, salvation, new creation, and theological anthropology. Following this trajectory, he identifies the problems it raises, and how the Scriptures speak to them. In particular, he addresses the problem of God's sovereignty in our rejection of him, God's reprobation of the wicked. On page 139 there is a long quote from Romans 9:6-19, but it is not well explained, and the context is underplayed.

Further work scholarly work on predestination is also at hand. Last year, Stephen Williams' Kevin Kantzer Lectures in Revealed Theology were published as: *The Election of Grace: a riddle without a resolution?*[251] His treatment is helpful. Indebted to him, and others, we need to seek what lies behind Paul's excitement about election in Ephesians 1, and his heart-rending cry in Romans 9:1-5.

Election is in the service of the fulfilment of God's promise to Abraham. In the Old Testament election is to service and privilege and knowledge and communion. Here it embraces Israel, tribes, individuals - Deuteronomy 7:6-11; 2 Samuel 7:1-29; Psalm 65:1-5 and Psalm 147. In the New Testament there are two new and key developments. Jesus Christ is *the* Elect One of God. And, for the first time, for the church and individuals, election is *to eternal life* - Ephesians 1:14, 20-23; John 10:27-30; Acts 13:48. In all of this, although God's decision is before the foundation of the world, election is never a remote, impersonal decree of a *deus ex machina*. Indeed, the *non-elect* Queen of Sheba rejoices and give thanks to God of Israel for the election of King Solomon (1 Kings 10:6-9)! God's election has entered into and works in time and history.

---

[251] Stephen Williams, *The Election of Grace: A Riddle Without a Resolution?* (Grand Rapids: Eerdmans, 2015).

Finally, in this brief statement, we need to note that in the New Testament, reprobation is *not* co-ordinated with election to life. As the wider context of Romans 9 makes clear, it is coordinated with the gospel offer that is universally and genuinely made. Reprobation is God's decision and action *in time* to judge sinful refusal of his good lordship and the real offer of salvation genuinely made, and it is a decision and action made to advance God's saving purpose (see especially Romans 9-11). These differentiations and observations offer greater clarity to Broughton's presentation.

In my opinion, predestination is best conceived of as uni-elemental, as election. Election is to faith (Acts 13:48). That is the stance of Article 17, and in the end, of Broughton himself.

In Summary

To summarise such a rich book risks presumption, but as indicated in the opening, I think we may say with some accuracy that three main, related terms characterise its chapters, and indeed, Broughton's work at large: God is *personal*, God is *other-person-centred*, and *relationship*. This is, as Broughton has carefully argued, the nub of the teaching of Holy Scripture.

An Awkward Moment: How I Tarnished the Knox Festschrift

Peter Jensen

My copy of *God who is Rich in Mercy,* the essays presented to Dr D. B. Knox, is inscribed by him 'For Peter Jensen in appreciation of the honour of his article and for his long friendship with Christian greetings Broughton Knox September 17 1986'.

Whenever I see this I groan. Let me tell you why.

The Festschrift was an excellent idea, excellently executed by Peter O'Brien and David Peterson, who were the editors. The title was good, the contributors honoured the man with significant essays, the book is handsome, the photo inside does him justice.

Dr Knox had not found leaving his role as Principal easy. Among other things, it was not simple to farewell him appropriately, as he was still the Principal when these things had to be organised and he appeared to be in two minds as to whether he could leave this to others or make suggestions himself. Likewise his feelings about a Diocesan farewell were, to say the least, ambivalent.

For those of us who deeply revered him, therefore, the Festschrift, hidden from his view until it was unveiled, as the custom is, would speak with a voice emphatic of our respect and love. Here was a man who had shaped us, reshaped the Diocese and created the modern College both physically and intellectually. His powerful ministry deserved a worthy tribute.

Imagine our dismay, then, when it became clear that one of the essays had wounded him deeply and it seemed as though for him the whole book was tarnished by the inclusion of this piece. And, all this was my fault.

What happened was this.

In our discussions about who should write for the Festschrift, I made the point that the volume would be an opportunity to introduce Broughton's theological thinking to a wider audience. He had published relatively little; he was not well known beyond Australia; he was better known for his lectures and the impact he had on the lives of students. And yet his ideas were biblical, with a creativity and freshness, a persuasiveness and a substance, that actually enabled us to face the challenges of modernity and post-modernity in a resolute yet flexible way. He was a thinker whose thoughts needed to be much better known. What better way than to have them weighed and explained in a book dedicated to his honour. It was a highly unusual proposal, but I managed to convince the editors that it was a worthy one.

Who should do this? I suggested the name of Robert Banks for several reasons. He was a very able scholar; he was one of the first of the cadre of student trained by Broughton in the early sixties; I knew that Broughton deeply respected him and would have had him on the Moore faculty had circumstances permitted. In my view, he had the fundamental sympathy for Broughton and knowledge of his theology suitable for this task, but was sufficiently detached from the College and the Diocese to be a credible witness. I was certainly not looking for an adoring exposition which would be out of place, but a critical examination which would show that Broughton's work was worthy of such study and robust enough to create dialogue.

Robert, then on leave in the UK for some months, was approached and agreed. He re-read Broughton's published works and produced the essay which appears in the volume under the title, 'The Theology of D.B. Knox – a preliminary estimate'.

In preparation for today, I have spoken to Robert Banks. Those of you who know him will attest to his personal warmth, integrity and care for people. He did what he was asked to do, and despite some stirring of misgiving by the Editors, the essay was included. I want to make it clear that no fault whatsoever may be attributed to Robert Banks or the editors for that matter. The essay does what I hoped for; it is not polemical, mischievous or malicious; it is properly critical, uncovering the strengths of the Knox theology while at the same time raising questions and offering dissent.

After indicating the necessary limitations of his essay and also the way in which he has seen development in Knox's work, Banks addresses *Main Preoccupations* which he identifies as God, Faith, the Bible and the Church; *Chief Contributions* which he sees to be Re-asserting Neglected

Truths and Providing fresh Insights, and, finally, *Key Weaknesses* which, to him, are in the area of Methodological Adequacy, Biblical Basis, Theological Range and Philosophical Outlook. He concludes with these words: 'If he taught us nothing else, David Broughton Knox made it impossible for us to settle for anything less than giving God his due, not as we but as God himself defines it. And it is this which constrains me to critique certain aspect of his theology and to raise these questions here. He, of all people, I think, will understand this.'[252]

But he did not. He did not understand it, not at all.

Broughton was hurt. For the person intended to be honoured, the Festschrift was tarnished, through my own thoughtlessness. Let me say how sorry I am that this was so; he was the last man I would have wished to harm in this way.

What went wrong?

First of all, I think I misunderstood the man and the moment. Robert Banks indicated to me in personal conversation, that in his own assessment Broughton enjoyed controversy and vigorous discussion, that he was secure in himself and that he was always developing in his thinking. I concur. I myself thought that Broughton would see that the essay was a tribute to him, precisely because it was properly critical. Here was the way of making his contribution far better known. He, of all people, enjoyed the cut and thrust of debate and argument and he was perfectly willing to change his mind on matters. Furthermore, to me, as one almost thirty years my senior, he seemed secure and strong. He had been in many public controversies and had not wilted.

But it is easy to misunderstand the generations ahead and behind you. It is easy to underestimate the toll of disagreement and debate. Broughton had committed himself to difficult and contested positions in church and culture. He may rightly have expected that in the bosom of his friends and in the book intended to honour him, peace may justly reign.

And the moment was not right. Stepping aside from the principalship was not easy. As can be seen from the founding of George

---

[252] Robert J. Banks, "The Theology of D.B. Knox—A Preliminary Estimate," in *God Who is Rich in Mercy*, ed. Peter T. O'Brien and David G. Peterson (Hombush West, N.S.W.: Lancer Books, 1986), 399.

Whitfield College, he was, like Moses, still capable of great and fruitful exertion. Furthermore, the conclusion of his tenure had created considerable personal turbulence. It was inevitably a time for reflection and for judgement – self-judgement of course, but inevitably the judgement of others. He was a controversial person and there were those only too willing to pass a negative judgement.

I think we rightly saw that this book would say to the world, here was a man worth listening to, here was a man who made a vast local, and in the end international, contribution, here was a man of theological stature; we do not want to lose his influence; we want to honour him and keep alive what he taught us. As Archbishop Robinson said in his beautifully written Appreciation, 'he is a repository of old-fashioned virtues and good manners. He is a very faithful friend, and it is no more than his due that he should be the recipient of this tribute from a company of distinguished scholars who know something of his worth.'

That says it all and that should have been enough. Yes, he was a man of ideas; yes, he enjoyed a good argument; yes, his mind was flexible; yes, he was secure in his God; but I had chosen the wrong forum and the wrong moment. I was impatient to share his legacy; he wanted this moment to enjoy and secure his legacy, not have it critiqued in such a way that he would have to explain and defend himself again.

What stung him? We must remember that Banks begins with an appreciation of the positives, although even there he interacts with them by way of review and modification. However, more than half his essay is devoted to the theme of the *Key Weaknesses,* which he labels Methodological Adequacy, Biblical Basis, Theological Range and Philosophical Outlook.

Given the time available, I am not going to do justice to Robert Banks – I am not expounding or personally responding to his criticisms. Nonetheless, to give the context is necessary. Bank's assessment runs along these lines: that the Knoxian theology was developed 'too independently of the wider world of theological discussion'.[253] His interaction with contemporary thought (and this includes contemporary culture) is sparse and selective. His critique of the historical-critical method of biblical interpretation (as illustrated by his dismissal of C.H.

---

[253] Ibid., 387.

Dodd on the parables) puts him outside virtually all scholarly discussion, discussion which may actually have helped him theologically.

Let me say how important this critique is to the discussion of the place of Knox in his own time and in the future. From the 1960s onward, there had been criticisms that he did not interact with contemporary theology, that he had not studied it and that he was, as a result, idiosyncratic, unaccountable, unscholarly and culturally outdated. Given the power of his local impact through Moore College, this continues to be a live issue. Is it true?

On the question of the biblical basis, Banks isolates three areas where he judges that the Knoxian theology is less than faithful to the text of Scripture: the primacy given to the power of God over the love of God, 'too rigid a distinction between the mercy and the "justice" of God', and thirdly the relation between word and Spirit, with too little emphasis being given to the Spirit in Knox's writings. In each of these areas Banks is seeking a better balance, a more careful integration.

In the area of theological range, Banks concentrates on what he calls Knox's 'unrelenting insistence on the role of the mind',[254] which he sees as a proper response to an emphasis on experience and encounter, but, once more as unbalanced. He cites our response to creation and the world of our feelings and emotions as areas which lack proper expression in the tone and content of Knox's writings. A second criticism in the same area is the concentration in Knox's work on doctrine at the expense of ethics, especially social as opposed to personal ethics. Knox reacts against the indigenisation of the gospel and 'there is very little attempt in his writings to come to grips with the particular beliefs, values, standards and language of people in Australian society all of which have been undergoing considerable change since the Second World War.'[255]

Turning, finally, to philosophical outlook, Banks relies fairly heavily on the one published critique of Knox up to that time, namely the work of Professor E. F. Osborne, who respectfully interacted with Knox's essay on propositional revelation, identifying it as an expression of 'empirical realism' and linking it to the influential philosopher, John Anderson of Sydney University. To Banks this is further evidence of the intellectualist approach of Knox, which in philosophical realism, 'tends to

---

[254] Ibid., 392.
[255] Ibid., 396.

reduce all things to one level... The experience of love, the beauty of landscape, the power of a vision, are all reduced to truth statements, when there is more to all of them than truth. Such an approach results in a monochrome view of the Bible. Its variety of literary forms and its varying moods tend to dissolve into a series of bare propositions; the roles of the imagination and emotion in understanding the Bible retreat as the intellect takes full charge.'[256]

And yet, as Banks then remarks, 'In any case, DBK does not seem to hold this view with complete consistency,' as he cites Knox's approach to faith.[257]

As I have re-read the Robert Banks' article, I think that, although it was commissioned in good faith and written without malice and with skill and respect, my judgement in commissioning it was poor. Robert Banks was understandably serious in his critique; he was not writing hagiography; but any hope of mine that this would create an appetite to know more about Broughton's theology and his contribution, was flawed. And yet, can something be saved even now?

I think something can and by a strange method.

Speaking as someone who has received a fair amount of public critique, journalistic and academic, I can understand what happened next. You look at the criticism; you assume its truthful elements; you bridle at its apparent injustice; you magnify any mistakes of fact; you ask if libel has occurred; you wonder at its misunderstandings; you hope that some friend will answer for you; you are caught between the impossibility of answering yourself and the fear that this will be the last word on your life's work. In other circumstances, indeed, it may be perfectly proper for a thinker to reply, correcting misunderstandings, accepting differences, expanding thoughts to explain and improve. Indeed, in other circumstances, this would have been an excellent opportunity for Knox to argue his case and bless us even more than he did. As he said himself: 'I hate having to justify myself but I am told I have an obligation to do so and no one else is in a position to.' And yet, given that this was a Festschrift in honour of him, how on earth could he respond?

---

[256] Ibid., 397.
[257] Ibid.

But he did.

Over the months and years that followed, he wrote 40 or so pages of notes on the Banks essay, and we still have them. I am sorry he had to do this, but I am so grateful that he did, because it gives us another, unpublished and hitherto unknown access to his remarkable mind. The notes are handwritten; my guess is that they were produced over several years; they are repetitive; they sometimes start as an essay and end as points; they don't amount to a sustained answer. But they are revealing. So, good has come from my regrettable error. And, for the remainder of this chapter I will begin an exploration of how he interacted with the critique that I foolishly engineered and Robert Banks innocently offered.

Broughton says a number of things in reply, some of which deal with details. But the main thrust of what he has to say is this:

At once, he makes clear his admiration of and affection for Robert Banks: 'I have a great affection for Robert Banks…He is a lovely man, fully committed to serving the Lord Jesus Christ. On more than one occasion it was my wish that he should join the Moore College faculty, but circumstances made a formal offer impossible.' Notwithstanding these sentiments, he makes a fairly trenchant set of responses which I have summarised in a threefold way: concerning the *sources* for which a study would need to be made; concerning his actual *methodology* as a theologian; concerning the actual *theology* he adhered to.

Sources

First, then, and this is a recurring theme, he thinks that Banks has failed to do justice to his theology because he has not surveyed the whole scope of it. In particular, he believes that you could only write about him if you had read his fifteen minute broadcast talks, his Certificate in Theology notes, his sermons and other articles and publications.

Now, this is an odd thing to say. I would not have thought that the Banks article needed to take into account what could be regarded as academic ephemera, material largely prepared for lay audiences and not submitted to any sort of peer review. In any case, Robert Banks was in the UK when he wrote it and did not have access to much of such material. But he clearly did not think it was in his remit to include that in his works except in a tangential way. That suits the academic context and would, I think, have been my own approach.

And yet, let us hear Broughton out on this. The value of the Banks criticism is that it draws out something about Broughton's idea of what he was doing theologically. In the first place, he regarded his public utterances as being real theology; he ascribed them a value which they may not have in a University, but here we may be seeing the limit of the mere academic. For Knox, the sermon in particular, exemplified what theology is about, namely the exposition of the word of God. It is academic because, properly done, it surpasses the academic and indeed engages the speaker in profound intellectual effort. In his own words, 'that I do not constantly refer to others in the papers which I write is due to my understanding of how theology should be written and what the objective is. The object is to make clear some aspect of the "whole counsel of God" and to see how it applies to our life.'

To accept this would then extend the range of Broughton's theological writings into the area of ethics and I think if you did so you would also begin to answer some of the Bank's hesitations about the nature of his ethics. In short, I accept that, when the time comes to move beyond the preliminary survey, it would not be inappropriate to take his writings and speeches into account, although, bearing in mind his capacity to speculate and change his mind it would also be right to sort the ephemeral from the considered.

Methodology

Our second concern, clearly related to the first, is methodological. I have already referred to the way in which Knox was criticised over many years for the paucity of his references to others in his theological speeches and writings. Does this mean that he had not read the classics and was not reading his contemporaries? Banks makes this same point effectively. How does Broughton respond?

Well, I am glad to say that he addresses this issue directly. Was he properly erudite? On his own account, yes he was; on his own account this is indispensable for the teacher of theology. He refers to his experience of hearing and meeting contemporary scholars and having access to the great libraries of the world. 'A theologian,' he writes, 'should be very well acquainted with the pivotal thinkers of the past and of the present (of which there are one or two). Their thought will enter into his own thinking but unless he is writing a history of theology, they will never be referred to by name.'

Whatever we may think of that as a method, I must also note the caveat he offers, that contemporary theologians write from a presuppositional base so different from classical theology that entering into dialogue is less than useful. Indeed, Banks quotes Knox dismissing virtually the whole of modern Biblical studies, specifically the work of C. H Dodd, since it is based on the historical-critical method. And yet, Knox reminds us that that he was in Dodd's seminar in Cambridge and he refers to him as a great scholar. It reminds me of his sterling defence of modern biblical scholarship in class one day when a student was dismissive of Dodd. I suggest that what we are dealing with here is not a form of anti-intellectualism or invincible ignorance, but rather a defence of Biblical authority and infallibility at a principal level.

In any case, the Banks article itself bears indirect testimony to Knox's knowledge of and place within the classical tradition. He was certainly theologically well informed. And, as reference to his fine doctoral thesis shows, he knew the arts of the academic world, including heavy citation in multiple footnotes, even though he was quite dismissive of PhD'ism as he called it, and the multiplication of references. He did not think that this indicated scholarship.

Two Further Observations

First, there was a theological reason for the lack of direct reference to others. So much systematic theology is built around conversations with other theologians or indeed with one or other of the traditions. Broughton's method was a deliberate decision to model a direct encounter with the word of God in the light of what others have said. 'My aim,' he said, '[is] to expound the underlying truth of reality in the mind of God and as reflected in the Bible the word of God.' In the end, this is what gave his classroom teaching such authority and this was a decision which served the expository preaching ministry which he was committed to further. He was in the pocket of no other theologian; he sought to understand and expound the word of God.

Second... and yet, in the end, it is not good enough. How can others follow this when they lack the erudition which is thus concealed? How can we all benefit from the words of others, such as the great C.H Dodd? And how can you best relate to the contemporary world of thought? Is there a way of indisputably serving the word first, but in conversation with others?

Theology

Robert Banks offers his critique of the Knox theology at several points such as mercy and justice, power and love, word and Spirit and Broughton makes a reply. In each case it would be profitable to think further with both scholars.

But I want to go to what I consider to be the heart of the matter – propositional revelation. You will remember that Banks sees Knox's adherence to this, connected to what you may call the over-intellectualisation of theology – its emotional and spiritual dryness.

At one level, he may be open to such a charge. The article he wrote on propositional revelation reveals his concern to defend the authority of the Bible in the modern context and hence his interaction with modern theology; but I think myself that it overstates its case. A more moderate claim could have sustained his argument more effectively. Furthermore, he completely denied any connection to John Anderson, personally or intellectually and denied also that he was a philosophically an empirical realist.

But, I believe that he could in fact defend himself against the charge. In part it is a matter of semantics; but in part also a view of Scripture which I think he received from William Tyndale. Tyndale was prepared to say 'God is his word', by which he meant that the connection between speech and the person, even in human relations, is so close that we relate to each other primarily through words, words which evoke trust and then the full range of obedience and emotions and joy in the Holy Spirit. I am my word; as you treat my words, so you treat me; your faith in me is as good as my word. Here I think, some of Bank's puzzlement about Knox on faith and Knox on relationships may have been resolved. And here was the secret of his preaching which was technically poor, only salvaged by being simple and actually filled with power for those who could hear. It was power based on simplicity based on profundity based on deep and original learning.

Conclusion

And so, we owe a great debt to Robert Banks and I thank him. My account of this episode is, I trust, not the slightest reflection on him; rather it is my *mea culpa*. But I hope that it can provoke that thesis which we need to complement the biography which Marcia Cameron has blessed us with, and the books produced by Matthias Media. And I hope that such a work will not be of mere historical interest but will set our friend free to speak again and powerfully as a good servant of the living God.

One last word.

The Knox legacy is in people and in institutions. Anyone who doubts his intellectual stature, or his profound grasp of the Christian faith, or his determination to see it in action in the world, or his academic prowess, need only look here and at George Whitfield College. He was a great teacher and a great strategist: with Donald Robinson and Noel Pollard, he built this library, insisting that there be no censorship. He welcomed scholars of quite different traditions to the College. He supervised the immense step forward in the academic standards of the College. He insisted that it be a community. He provided for the indigenous faculty. His teaching set us sufficiently free from denominational traditionalism that we were in fact ready for the new Australia that was born in his time and has emerged since.

He was a great missionary; he was a great thinker; he was a great Australian, and we thank God for him.

Legacy 2: Moore College

Broughton Knox, Theological Education and the Modern Moore College

Mark D Thompson

David Broughton Knox (1916–94) took up his responsibilities as Principal of Moore Theological College, Sydney on 1 March 1959. He would remain in office until February 1985, the longest tenure as principal in the College's now 160 year history. Although thirty years on we might still not have quite enough historical perspective to make the judgment, it is almost certain that his has also been the most influential principalship in the history of the College. William Hodgson set the agenda for an evangelical theological college in the 1850s, T. C. Hammond recovered the strongly evangelical character of its education in the 1930s and 1940s after a decade in which it had begun to wander. Nevertheless, it is generally recognised that Broughton Knox raised the academic standard and positioned the College as an institution capable of making a significant contribution on the world stage. His legacy as a theological educator extends far beyond Moore College of course. However, in almost every facet of its life, the modern Moore College has been shaped by his vision.

It is worth mentioning that Broughton's shaping influence on the College goes back long before March 1959. He was in fact first appointed to the Moore College faculty in March 1947, following discharge from the Royal Australian Navy, in which he had spent the last months of the Second World War (he had been with the Royal Naval Volunteer Reserve during the D Day operations). The College was never far from his heart and mind from that point on. Even in retirement he taught theology at the College for a few years and during his years in South Africa his interest in all that was going on at Moore continued unabated.

What we must, therefore, more properly recognise as an over 40 year active association with the College (not just a 26 year one), was punctuated by three important periods of leave, during each of which he returned to England. These periods of research and writing provide important markers in his general theological thinking and his thinking about theological education in particular. Between 1951 and 1953 he was in Oxford, researching towards his DPhil. During that time, he taught New Testament at Wycliffe Hall. In 1968 he was a given a sabbatical during which he researched the English Reformation, in particular on the Lord's Supper, and then visited, on his own count, around 40 theological colleges and seminaries in the UK and America (and spoke with the staff of around 20 others). He also attended a Conference of Anglican Principals in Oxford in September that year. Then, in 1980, he returned to England, spending quite some time at Tyndale House in Cambridge. There he finished his little book on the Lord's Supper from Wycliffe to Cranmer.

Marcus Loane discerned subtle shifts in Broughton's way of speaking, or the key terms he used in describing the Christian life, after each of these periods of study. Writing in 1988 Marcus remembered,

> On his return from England in 1953, Faith was the keyword in his teaching; he liked to say that the exercise of Faith is Worship. After 1968, the keyword was Fellowship; the main purpose of a Christian assembly is to enter into Fellowship with the Lord of the church and with its members. After 1980, it was Relationship; the ideal of Relationship in the Triune Godhead is the perfect pattern for His people.[258]

The context of this reminiscence was Marcus's gentle criticism that while 'Broughton's mind was very subtle... he had a tendency to crystallize his thinking in short dogmatic statements which over-simplified the situation'. Even so, the criticism was further tempered with the observation 'the thinking that lay behind such keywords was acute'.[259]

Just as significant, though, was the fact that each stay abroad prompted reflection upon the task of theological education. Upon his return from the leave of 1968, he provided a report to the Moore College Committee which was very largely a blueprint for the modern College. In

---

[258] Marcus Loane, *These Happy Warriors: Friends and Contemporaries* (Blackwood, S.A.: New Creations Publications, 1988). 61.
[259] Ibid.

1980, while in Cambridge, he put together 'Some Notes on Principles for Conducting Training for the Ministry', later published as an appendix to the little volume *Sent By Jesus: Some Aspects of Christian Ministry Today*.[260]

Before attempting to make some broader observations about his approach to theological education and its impact on the shape of Moore College even more than twenty years after his death, it will be helpful to take a brief look at what he did and what he wrote after those periods overseas and to add to them, in its place, the crucial moment when he took over the leadership of the College. Trawling through four decades of Moore College Committee minutes reveals Broughton's remarkably consistent and coherent vision for the College, even if that vision continues to expand as the years progress.

March 1947: The First Flush

Broughton's first period on the full-time faculty of the College began in March 1947 and it appears he was brim full of ideas right from the start. His name appears regularly in the minutes of the Moore College Committee that year, with a steady stream of letters from Mr D. B. Knox suggesting changes. In March he suggested that letters be used after the names of the faculty in formal documents. In August 1947 he suggested a new system for examining ordination candidates that included a two or three day residential conference for the candidates and the Board of Reference. In September he suggested an annual grant to cover the cost of periodicals and in October he wrote about academic conditions at the College. In November he put forward a proposal to invite resident teaching staff to become members of the Committee. The next month he put forward another proposal, this time for a scholarship for university graduates, to be named the Lukyn Williams Scholarship. Then, in April the next year, he wrote to the Committee about the Library, suggesting space should be provided ultimately for 100,000 volumes and that there be an annual grant from the Committee of £100 for the purchase of books.[261]

---

[260] Knox, *Sent by Jesus*, 74–79.

[261] Each of these proposals is documented in the Moore College Committee Minutes for that year, held in the Donald Robinson Library at Moore College.

All of this is evidence that from the very first moments of his formal association with the College Broughton had plans for its future. Perhaps it helped that in the second half of 1947 and all of 1948 the Principal, Archdeacon T. C. Hammond, was on leave in England and Marcus Loane, Broughton's brother-in-law, was in the chair. Clearly Marcus appreciated Broughton's energy and willingness to make constructive suggestions. After all, in that same period Marcus proposed a stipend increase and that Broughton be titled 'Dean of the College'! However that may have been, Broughton's proposals ranged over academic matters, administrative matters, the library, student finances, and the process of selecting appropriate candidates for ordination. All this from the most junior member of the faculty at the time without any thought of waiting until he had settled into the post.

February 1954: Innovations in a New Era

In November 1950, after four years of teaching at Moore, Broughton and his new wife Ailsa left for his doctoral studies in Oxford. Upon his return from doctoral studies, Broughton took up the post of Vice Principal under the new Principal, Marcus Loane. He brought back to Moore College some of the experience he had gained during the years of study in the University, his teaching at Wycliffe Hall, and his post as curate at St Aldates in Oxford. One very significant change was the replacement of the College's Annual Convention with a College Mission in various parishes.[262] He even wrote his own tract for use in those missions.[263] Surprisingly, Dr D B Knox doesn't feature prominently in the College Committee minutes in the mid to late 1950s. A young family and a heavy teaching and administrative load no doubt kept him occupied.

March 1959: Taking the Reins

Another new chapter in Broughton's involvement with the College began in March 1959, not following another trip overseas, but rather when he took over from Marcus Loane as Principal. It was a new chapter for the College too! Marcia Cameron's biography includes a comment from Alan Cole on the three Principals he knew well: T. C. Hammond, Marcus

---

[262] Loane, *These Happy Warriors*, 58.
[263] Unfortunately, the Moore College Committee minutes for 1954 and 1955 are missing from the collection housed in the Donald Robinson Library. These may well have indicated other suggestions from the new Vice Principal.

Loane and Broughton Knox. He described T. C. as 'in many ways a traditional old-style, old-fashioned theologian, whose roots were very much in the great evangelical protestant tradition'. Marcus was similar and 'would have felt himself at home with any of the great evangelical bishops of the Anglican Church of the last century'. And Broughton? 'I think Broughton was very thoroughly a Reformation man'.[264]

The changes came quickly when Broughton became principal. In August 1959 he proposed to the Committee that the College course be extended to four years, at first by inviting 5 or 6 third year students to tutor first year students and begin to study for the Th. Schol. and the Diploma of Religious Education. Yet in that very proposal he made clear this was a pilot scheme for a full fourth year, which might begin in 1961. One of those who was invited into that first full fourth year was a young Peter O'Brien! Broughton tied to this proposal his conviction that 'the College must take active measures for training its own future teaching staff'.[265] This was a monumental change in the College program that was to bear dividends in the decades to come.

Two months later Broughton provided the Committee with a summary of a talk he had given at the Old Students' Reunion on 23rd September:

> The Principal spoke on 'The Outlook on Theological Education'. He mentioned first of all the pressure on the curriculum, which required a list of priorities to be arrived at — foremost amongst which must be the knowledge of the content and themes of the Bible, and of methods of exposition; as the knowledge of God was the foundation of all Christian life — individual and parish.
>
> The British Ideal in theological training was to train and discipline the mind of the student, so that he could be his own educator throughout life. The Americans were inclined to stress the need of learning techniques; but if this tendency was not carefully controlled, these

---

[264] 'R. A. Cole Interview 28 May 2003' in Cameron, *Enigmatic Life*, 162.
[265] Moore College Committee Minutes of the meeting held 20 August 1959.

techniques would engross the curriculum. Techniques must always be the handmaiden to knowledge.

The Principal then spoke about the future of theological science in Australia, and stressed the key position that Moore College held in the development of this.[266]

Many of these accents would be recognisable to his students as characteristically Broughtonian: the prime and central place of the Bible, the even more foundational concept of the knowledge of God, the insistence that technique must remain a handmaiden to knowledge.

The completion of a new dining room in 1961 made space for a new library reading room and the first steps towards building a substantial library. Broughton had outlined his vision years before but now was able to begin to shape it in reality.[267] In 1962 he returned to his prior concern for the training of future theological leaders. In August he wrote:

> Next to the building up of an adequate and qualified staff, and the development of the College library for research for Masters' and Doctors' degrees, I believe that the provision of a travelling scholarship for Moore College graduates is of the utmost importance and urgency. If our young leaders are to take their proper place in the Australian Church in the future, they must have the opportunity of travelling overseas. This is expensive, especially in the theological realm, for in the realm of organisation and technique a quick trip overseas often suffices, but for those who are to make a contribution in the important field of theological leadership, whether strictly academic, or in the broad area of Councils of the Church, a longer stay overseas is necessary for study under overseas teachers. Such overseas studies must as a

---

[266] Included in Moore College Committee Minutes October 1959, over the initials D.B.K.
[267] Moore College Committee Minutes of the meeting of 21 September 1961.

general rule be undertaken when a man is young, and its full results are not seen for 10 or 15 years.[268]

Here was one of the first expositions of a strategy for Moore developing its own future faculty, a practice that would serve the College well for the rest of the twentieth century and into the twenty-first. Broughton would return again and again to the question of postgraduate scholarships. On one occasion he reported to the Committee that he had 'put a notice in the church press' and then remarked '[t]he action I confess was unilateral'.[269]

During the course of 1963 Broughton explored the idea of appointing two professorships at the College and with the Committee's good will he approached Dr Leon Morris, then in the UK, to see if he would be the first of them. In August he received a reply:

> I am more honoured than I can readily say at your invitation to become Moore's first professor. And I like the outline you give of the duties entailed in the post. I am sure that this is a great step forward, and it could mean a great deal for the promotion of biblical scholarship in Australia.
>
> However you will doubtless have heard by the time this reaches you that I have accepted the invitation of the Ridley College Council to become Principal. Had your invitation come along before that from the Ridley men, or even while I was considering it, who can tell what the result would have been?[270]

In the next year he once again pushed for 'the development of a Post-graduate School of Theology at Moore College', which would include: firstly, 'two professorships to be held by men who have already made their mark as evangelical scholars and who could use their time to guide

---

[268] Moore College Committee Minutes of the meeting of 16 August 1962.

[269] Moore College Committee Minutes of the meeting of 21 February 1963.

[270] Moore College Committee Minutes of the meeting of 15 August 1963. (The issue of the two professorships had first been raised in the Minutes of the meeting of 20 June 1963).

research students'; secondly, 'the provision of postgraduate scholarships to enable say the two brightest students in any year to continue their studies ... to take their master's degree'; and thirdly, 'a Post-graduate Travelling Scholarship to be awarded, say once every two years on a two year tenure, to enable the more promising students to go overseas to study for two or three years for a doctorate'.[271] Three months later he was arguing for 'a post graduate fund for three objectives': (1) two residential post-graduate scholarships; (2) an overseas travelling scholarship; and (3) 'a fund to enable the College to invite distinguished overseas teachers to be visiting professors at Moore College'.[272]

It is particularly noteworthy that in this same period that gives ample evidence of his interest in extending the academic reach of the College in the direction of postgraduate studies, Broughton gave concentrated attention to the College's program for lay theological education. The College had been formally involved in lay education since 1941 when Principal T. C. Hammond initiated the Sydney Preliminary Theological Certificate (S.P.T.C.). Originally this had been a course taught in the evenings, with the lecturer supplying notes to those who attended. The two year program had become the basic requirement for those who sought a lay reading license in the diocese. Broughton saw the opportunity to reach more people and to strengthen the churches. He dreamed of a program of theological education for lay people that paralleled to some degree the Th.L., which at that time was the basic qualification for ordination in the Diocese of Sydney. In 1963 he invited Rev B. Ward Powers to join the faculty with the specific brief of implementing his (Broughton's) vision for external studies. A correspondence course was developed over the next four years which included thirty subjects — thirty sets of notes (ten lessons in each with guided reading and an examination) were produced between 1964 and 1967! In time this course would have an international impact, being studied in places as diverse as England, Chile, China, and Tanzania. Here is further evidence of Broughton's conviction that the study of theology was properly a service to the churches, not the exclusive activity of an academic guild.

---

[271] Moore College Committee Minutes of the meeting of 18 June 1964.

[272] Moore College Committee Minutes of the meeting of 17 September 1964.

February 1969: A Vision for the Future

Broughton had been working at Moore College for fourteen years after his return from doctoral studies before he received his first sabbatical. He spent a year travelling from one theological college to another, taking note of how things were being done and how they worked and engaging in extended conversation with fellow Principals. He then attended the Conference of Anglican Principals in Oxford in September 1968. One of the very first things he did on his return in February 1969 was to write a report for the College Committee, complete with recommendations.

Quite early on in this 23 page report, Broughton remarked, 'My visit overseas has not modified in any way the basic objectives of Moore College, but rather strengthened the conviction of their soundness'.[273] What were those basic objectives, as he understood them at that time? He continued,

> The (*sic*) remain, firstly, the thorough investigation of the contents and principles of the Bible as God's revelation of His relationship to us and of our relation to one another, and the teaching of these to those who seek to fit themselves to fulfil God's calling to be pastors and teachers in the congregation. We do this in a Church of England context, though not exclusively to Church of England students, and along with this, the imparting of technical skills, especially in preaching and teaching, as time and opportunity allow. Secondly, there is the co-ordinate objective of the creation of a Christian fellowship in which its members may grow in Christian experience and grace, through prayer, exposition of the Word of God, exhortation and Christian fellowship.[274]

We might summarise these two objectives as teaching/training on the one hand and Christian growth on the other. Characteristically, Broughton saw the teaching of the Bible, or the exposition of the Word of God, as critical in the achievement of *both* objectives.

---

[273] D. B. Knox, 'Report to the Moore College Committee by the Principal, February 1969', 4, included in the Moore College Committee Minutes for 1969.
[274] Knox, 'Report', 4.

The body of this report is a systematic account of what he observed going on in the colleges in the UK and America, occasionally digressing to make suggestions for Moore College, under the following headings:

1. Student Life — he lamented the impact of a new accent on 'freedom';
2. Teaching Methods — he recommended extending the tutorial system then in use for first year students;
3. Practical Work —he outlined the differing British and American models;
4. Finance — once again he contrasted the English experience with its significant reliance upon grants from the Advisory Council for the Church's Ministry and the American experience with various fundraising programs;
5. Administration
6. Post-graduate Facilities
7. Relationship to Universities

When Broughton turned to talk about Moore College and his recommendations for the future, he began: 'Moore College was founded by a trust deed which became effective in 1840 for the education of Protestant youth according to the principles of the Church of England in Australia'.[275] He cheekily preferred to stress this date than 1856, the date when the College opened and took its first students. As much as any reason, it seems, this date situated the College as the first higher education institution in the Australia — the University of Sydney was only established in 1850, ten years later!

The vision he wished to put before the Committee in 1969 was larger than anything before:

> We should use every endeavour to build in Sydney a theological school based on evangelical biblical principles which would serve the whole of Australia and also South East Asia ... The primary obligation of the College is to

---

[275] Knox, 'Report', 11.

serve the Diocese, but its trust deeds are larger than the Diocese.[276]

He then sought to outline what would be needed to realise this vision:[277]

1. A coherent under-graduate curriculum under the control of the College faculty, of four years duration, leading to the College's own graduating degree.
2. The development of the library. He pointed out that all the American colleges he visited devoted at least 10% of their budget each year to the library.
3. The forming of the faculty into departments (Old Testament, New Testament, Christian Thought, Pastoral and Practical Theology).
4. The College should aim 'to build up the staff to a ratio of one to twelve of the total number of full-time students taught.
5. An enlarged committee with subcommittees.
6. The establishment of a Division of Ministry 'responsible for giving or arranging lectures in homiletics, counselling, conduct of services, parochial ministry, discussion with students before and after practice sermons, College missions, College convention, hospital courses, catechist work'.

He then went on to speak about Faculty Structure, Grades and Scales of Remuneration, the establishment of a scheme for sabbatical leave, which would exist 'to improve the efficiency of the teaching staff'.[278] Other observations were made about 'part-time theological courses for older men', 'post ordination training', and 'in service training for clergy'. This, he realised, would all need to be serviced by a strengthened academic registry.[279] He also made suggestions about buildings and public relations.

In the series of recommendations which follow, six stand out as significant given both the moment and the College's future:[280]

---

[276] Knox, 'Report', 12.
[277] Knox, 'Report', 12–15.
[278] Knox, 'Report', 18.
[279] Knox, 'Report', 18–19.
[280] Knox, 'Report', 22–24.

BROUGHTON KNOX, THEOLOGICAL EDUCATION AND THE MODERN MOORE COLLEGE

1. 'Enrol men and women students on an equality though only providing residential qualification for men students at present'.
2. Provide two basic courses: (1) 'a four year course after matriculation with its own integrated curriculum ... This course to have an exit diploma to be called B.Th. in due course'; (2) 'a three year course without matriculation necessarily being required, leading to the new Diploma of Theology of the A[ustralian] C[ollege of] T[heology] (or if a matriculant, the Th. L. [with Greek]).
3. Establish a post graduate course ... 'its exit diploma should at some future time be called an M.Th'
4. Adopt the aim of a ratio of one staff member to 12 full-time students.
5. Organise teaching staff into three departments (Old Testament, New Testament, Christian Thought).
6. Approve the establishment of a Division of Christian Ministry.

Later in 1969 Broughton elaborated on his proposal for a Division of Ministry, producing an extended statement on the nature of ministry training:

> In training a man or a woman for a life-time ministry of the Word of God within the church, the fundamental equipment is a thorough knowledge of the mind of God as He has revealed it to us. This knowledge of God's revelation of His character and His relations to us, cannot be obtained by common sense reflection on life but must be taught generation by generation from the written word of God. In our present situation the men and women who offer for the work of the ministry come with altogether too shallow a knowledge to sustain them in a true ministry for the rest of their life, and our present structures do not allow sufficient time to the average person for learning during the course of his professional life. Consequently, the period of College training is of utmost importance and the great bulk of the time available should be devoted to the study of the revelation of God, the understanding of its principles and its content. A knowledge of God's revelation is the basic preparation for the work of the ministry. A course directed to gaining this knowledge is

> the same in content whether the student intends to be a minister, or to be a well-informed Christian layman.
>
> The work of the professional ministry in our present age does, however, require insights and skills in addition to a knowledge of God's revelation. Though it is true that these insights and skills can be picked up if need be by an intelligent person during the course of his ministry such a method would entail a good deal of painful learning, and mistakes which may perhaps injure those to whom he is ministering. Consequently, it is desirable to equip with professional skills and insights the embryonic minister as far as possible, so long as there is no encroaching on the necessary minimum time to be given to obtaining the more primary qualification of a knowledge of God's revelation.[281]

Broughton was certainly committed to improving academic standards at the College. Of that there can be no doubt. However, he was just as concerned that this theological rigour serve the end of gospel ministry in the churches. His institution of a Division of Ministry at the College was borne out of a commitment to the priority of raising up leaders for the churches. The postgraduate program too served that purpose rather than any orientation towards the theological academy. This same commitment was further evidenced by the extension of the external studies program with the revival of the evening lectures for lay men and women in 1976, leading to the award of a Diploma of Biblical Studies. This meant there were two avenues of study for those who were not able to engage in the full-time program and were not intending to train for full-time ministry: the correspondence course and the evening course. Broughton knew that strong gospel ministry in the churches relied not just on ordained leadership with a deep and extensive immersion in 'the whole counsel of God', but also on lay leadership that was itself theologically informed and shaped.

1980: Principled Reflection on the Task

The 1980 study leave in Tyndale House, Cambridge, as we have already noted, provided Broughton with a further opportunity to set forth in

---

[281] Moore College Committee Minutes of the meeting on 13 June 1969.

writing his vision for the College. The very heading he used for his paper is instructive. He did not entitle it 'Principles for conducting theological education' but rather 'Principles for conducting training for the ministry'. As a matter of firm conviction he did not consider theological education to have a life of its own, as something somehow separate or distinct from 'training for the ministry'. In all his efforts to improve academic standards and prepare those who could in time provide theological leadership, his focus remained on ministry rather than the academy. He knew very well the danger of an unanchored search for academic recognition for individuals and for institutions. The plethora of 'once-evangelical' colleges and seminaries around the world remains a testimony to that danger.

The document he prepared is just a sketch really, but it provides an insight into what he thought mattered near the close of his time as Principal of the College. He began with the selection of entrants. They must have (1) 'a true commitment to Christ as Lord'; (2) 'personal gifts which enable them to relate naturally to other people'; (3) 'intellectual ability'; and (4) 'a call to preach the gospel'. He then turned to the curriculum, which he first described in terms of what today we would call graduate attributes. On the completion of the four year course, students will:

1. 'have a grasp of the contents of the whole Bible as God's infallible Word and its teaching, so as to grasp the whole counsel of God';
2. 'understand the Bible as a unified whole and apprehend the concepts of the mind of God revealed in it'; and
3. have come into 'deeper fellowship with God' and 'be equipped to bring others into the same knowledge of him'.[282]

He then listed elements of the curriculum:

1. Biblical languages — at least 10 chapters of the Hebrew Bible and 100 chapters of the Greek New Testament;
2. Systematic biblical theology and Christian ethics — including the reading of 'certain designated Christian classics' (e.g. Calvin's *Institutes*);

---

[282] Knox, *Sent by Jesus*, 74–75.

3. Church History — an aid to understanding the modern situation in which the Christian faith is to be lived and proclaimed;
4. Philosophy — i.e. the various ways in which human existence has been apprehended;
5. Liturgiology — biblical principles guiding what Christians do when they come together to meet with Christ;
6. Pastoral counselling — a subdivision of Christian ethics since counselling is a duty that all Christians have to each other; and
7. Communication technology and praxis — an introduction to the practical art of conveying the Christian message by ministers of the Word.[283]

Having listed these seven elements Broughton returned to his most basic conviction: 'If students are not taught the whole counsel of God during their college course, most will not pick it up later as an integrated whole on which to base their ministry. Therefore teaching this has priority, if time is short'.[284]

Next he turned to the faculty, insisting they be persons 'devoted to the lordship of Christ, heavenly-oriented, fully committed to the infallibility of Holy Scripture and convinced that a knowledge of God through the Bible is the source of Christian living and ministry'.[285] Here he repeated something said many times and in many places: 'The quality of the teaching faculty may well be regarded as the primary principle for the conducting of the college'.[286]

The next principle concerned the library: 'A good library will support a good faculty and draw a good, studious student body'.[287] Then he returned to the ideal staff student ratio, insisting on no less than 12 members of the faculty and 'no less than one full-time member (or equivalent) to ten students (or eleven if student numbers are large), if students are to be given proper pastoral and tutorial care, and the faculty are to have time to deepen their own Christian knowledge'.[288]

---

[283] Ibid., 75–76.
[284] Ibid., 76.
[285] Ibid.
[286] Ibid., 77.
[287] Ibid.
[288] Ibid.

The final principle he mentioned was the formation of the 'spiritual life' through prayer and teaching. Here he mentioned the place of chapel, prayer groups and involvement in a Christian congregation on Sundays. The development of Christian character and habits of discipleship occurs within the context of fellowship and service. Yet the fundamental point of reference for Broughton was not fellowship in abstraction but life with God as he has made himself known in his word. This is borne out in one of the final statements of the paper, yet another characteristic description of the task viewed as a whole:

> Since everything in life is related to God, every subject in the curriculum should be related to God. Some will be more closely related to God in his relationships in himself and to his creation than others but all the lectures should have a teaching element of 'God's whole counsel' and consequently will not only stimulate the mind but also affect the heart, the conscience and the will.[289]

At each of these points (1947, 1954, 1959, 1969, 1980) the vision was clear and remarkably coherent. It undoubtedly grew and specific points of application emerged at various points throughout this period, but the core principles and perspectives remained. So how should we encapsulate Broughton Knox's vision for theological education?

The Knox Vision

Theological

Broughton's vision for theological education was itself deeply theological. It had to do, first and foremost, with his understanding of who God is and how he relates to the world. As we have just seen, Broughton viewed the chief business of a theological college as the knowledge of God, understood, characteristically, as fellowship with God. To know God is to be in fellowship with him. It is not something abstract but something deeply personal. God himself determines how he is known and the context in which his creatures grow in knowledge of him. Jesus put it this way in Matthew 11:27 — 'All things have been handed over to me by my Father, and no one knows the Son except the Father, and no one knows the Father except the Son and anyone to whom the Son chooses to reveal him'. At every point of human existence we are confronted with the

---

[289] Ibid., 78.

sovereignty of God: in creation, in redemption, and at this point too, the revelation of himself. God is known only as he reveals himself. He cannot be known around or behind his revelation. So the means by which God has chosen to make himself known must be central to the vision of a college which has as its goal knowing God and making God known. This is why Broughton placed such an emphasis on the Bible in the entire life of the College, not just its curriculum.

Biblical

We have already seen that Broughton regularly appealed to the words of Paul in Acts 20:27, 'I did not shrink from declaring to you the whole counsel of God'. In the very first lecture given in this building, Peter Jensen spoke of this as one of Broughton's 'favourite biblical references'.[290] Broughton wanted all who taught and studied in this College to be saturated with Scripture. It was to be the reference point in every lecture, no matter what the particular subject. The Moore College reflex was to be 'what does the Bible say?'[291]

I remember that in his last years as Principal, at the very end of one academic year, he invited students to sign up to a personal commitment to read the whole of the Bible through during the long vacation. He undertook to do the same. It was an indication of where the centre of gravity in our studies was to lie. Friends and colleagues have remarked that it was not unusual to see him sitting in the Principal's Garden quietly reading his Bible (usually his beloved Revised Version of 1885) or walking around in circles with his hands clasped behind his back as he prayed.

In 1990 he sketched a response to a published critique of his theology.[292] He had been accused of developing his theological method too independently of the wider world of theological discussion'.[293] The presenting evidence was, as he put it, 'I am not constantly citing and

---

[290] P. F. Jensen, "Broughton Knox on Training for Ministry," in *D. Broughton Knox: Selected Works*, ed. Tony Payne (Sydney: Matthias Media, 2000). 18.

[291] Ibid., 19.

[292] See Peter Jensen's contribution to this volume.

[293] Banks, "Preliminary Estimate," 387.

footnoting references to contemporary scholars'. Broughton was indignant. After all, had not the author of the critique, in the very critique itself, cited multiple examples of his familiarity with contemporary theological scholarship?[294] Hadn't he, Broughton, championed the growth of the Moore College library, filled to the rafters with biblical and theological scholarship from all persuasions and perspectives? But if that was true, and it was, why didn't he make much of classical or contemporary authors in his teaching and writing? His explanation gave further insight into his perspective, not just on theological education but on the discipline of theology itself.

> If I do not normally constantly refer to them in the pages of what I write, it is due to my understanding of how theology should be written, or what the objective is. The objective is to make clear some aspect of 'the whole counsel of God', and to then see how it applies to our life. True theology is an explanation of God's revelation. Therefore, there should be constant references to holy Scripture to assure the reader that what is being said is well grounded; but there is only need for an occasional reference to a writer in the last half-generation ... Every word in the Bible has been spoken to us by God, as our Lord and St Paul say explicitly. What God has spoken to us through these words is the task of the theologians to understand and make clear ...[295]

Important for understanding his tenacious advocacy of the primacy of the Bible is the way he refused to think of the word of God in isolation from the God who speaks it, the Bible from the one who gave it to us. He would sometimes use the aphorism, 'God is his word' and it appeared from time to time in examinations: 'God is his word. Discuss'. This was not bibliolatry or anything like that. It was rather an insight into something much more fundamental, and it is one that can be found, among others,

---

[294] E.g. Ibid., 377, 378, 381.
[295] D. B. Knox, 'The "Apologia Pro Theologica Mea": Robert Banks — A Reply' (unpublished paper, held by Matthias Media, dated 27 February 1990), 4, 7.

in the writings of William Tyndale, as Peter Jensen has recently shown.[296] In his 1990 *Apologia* Broughton wrote,

> But the Bible is not a thing in itself. There is only God and those to whom God spoke. The Bible is God speaking to us — one entity; and our receiving his word which we hear and respond to — the second entity. It is the same when two human friends speak to each other. There are two entities, the two friends. Their words are them. With God, the word he speaks to us is him, utterly truthful, inerrant and infallible ...[297]

Broughton Knox's conviction about the central place of the Bible in every aspect of theological education was a subset of his conviction that it has a central place in every aspect of the Christian life. This was far from some obscurantist fundamentalism. It was borne of deep reflection upon the nature of God as the one who addresses his people at this point. The Bible is 'God's personally directed speech'.[298] Yet it was also tied to his convictions about the nature of Christian ministry. After he had retired from Moore College, he wrote a report on theological education for the Synod of the Church of England in South Africa (CESA) in which he spelt this out.

> The minister of the congregation is the teacher of God's Word to the congregation. This is his main task. He will have other duties and opportunities of service as a Christian, but his main task is that of teacher. He is to open up the Word of God, so that the congregation can see what the verse, or the paragraph or the chapter or the

---

[296] P. F. Jensen, "God and the Bible," in *The Enduring Authority of the Christian Scriptures*, ed. D. A. Carson (Grand Rapids: Eerdmans, 2016), 477–496. The reference in Tyndale's writings is: 'God is nothing but his law and his promises; that is to say, that which he biddeth thee to do, and that which he biddeth thee believe and hope. God is but his word, as Christ saith, John viii. "I am that I say unto you"; that is to say, That which I preach am I; my words are spirit and life. God is that only which he testifieth of himself; and to imagine any other thing of God than that is damnable idolatry.' W. Tyndale, "The Obedience of a Christian Man," in *William Tyndale: Doctrinal Treatises*, ed. H. Walter (Cambridge: Parker Society, 1848), 146–147.

[297] Knox, 'Apologia', 7–8.

[298] Jensen, "Knox on Training," 19.

Book, or even the Bible as a whole, on which he is preaching, is actually saying. In this way the minister's words, being plainly seen to be what God is saying to the hearer, is received into the mind as God's word, and so reaches the conscience of the believer, suffuses his emotions, moves his will and issues in a godly life — friendship with God and loving actions towards others.

The minister is the teacher. This was our Lord's ministry. 'Teacher' was the title the people gave him and which he accepted. It was Paul's ministry. He told the Ephesians amongst whom he ministered for three years that he had taught them in their homes and publically 'the whole counsel of God'.

And it is the teaching ministry that has been entrusted to the modern minister. As Paul told Timothy, what you have received from me in association with many others, do you hand on to faithful men who are able to teach others also'. The modern minister of the congregation is the last in this line of apostolic succession in the teaching ministry, and it is his great privilege and task in his turn to teach others also 'the whole counsel of God'.[299]

Broughton knew full-well that theological colleges around the world were not as focussed on the revelation of God in the Bible. He was well aware of the smorgasbord approach to teaching theology, which surveyed a topic in the thought of one great theologian after another. He had watched others replace biblical theology with historical theology without ever really acknowledging that was what they were doing. So although he knew and understood what is today often referred to as 'the theological tradition', he resolutely called us back again and again to what God has to say — infinitely more interesting than what Augustine, Calvin, Barth or Knox have to say. Theological education, if it is to live up to its name and be truly theological, must be determinedly biblical.

---

[299] D. B. Knox, 'Report by David Broughton Knox to the Executive of the Synod of the Church of England in South Africa on Theological Education' (1986), 1, quoted in ibid., 17.

Relational

The third general aspect of Broughton's vision for theological education was his commitment to the importance of relationships and community as the context in which all teaching and learning is done. It has often been said that he regarded the dining room and the common rooms as just as important as the classroom and the chapel. If theological education is more than simply conveying information, but building convictions and shaping character as well — in short if it is about knowing God and enjoying fellowship with God — then it is not something that can appropriately be done in isolation outside of a learning community. Broughton was not denying that we can think about God or study theology on our own.[300] Nevertheless, an effective theological education, or better, 'training for the ministry', takes place in a society of fellow learners. Relationships are not incidental to the task but instead are integral to it.

Fundamentally this aspect too arose from his understanding of the nature of God. As he said in *The Everlasting God,*

> Through the revelation of the Trinity we learn that the living God, the good and true God, is a God who has relationship within Himself and that the values of relationships ultimately belong to reality in its most absolute form. In the light of this doctrine, personal relationships are seen to be ultimate, are seen to be the most real things that are.[301]

The College Broughton shaped was, and is, a fellowship first of all, a community of disciples learning together. Warm personal relationships are its basic currency: between the faculty, between faculty and students, between the students themselves. Of particular importance was the sustained personal engagement of teacher and student. You'll remember his rationale for a 1:10 faculty/student ratio in 1980: to ensure 'students are to be given proper pastoral and tutorial care' and also to allow the faculty time 'to deepen their own Christian knowledge'.

---

[300] Ibid., 23.
[301] D. Broughton Knox, *The Everlasting God* (Welwyn: Evangelical Press, 1982). 51–52.

This proper, theologically driven, preoccupation with relationships helps to explain Broughton's dogged advocacy of residence and the importance he placed on College meals. The principle of residence needed defending again and again in Broughton's time and since. It is very costly both for the College and for the student. Nevertheless, living alongside one another, learning to embody what is taught together, asking questions, sharing struggles, challenging for greater clarity — all of this was vital in Broughton's vision. Furthermore, study in cohorts (the alternative to a suite of electives in each year) built relationships which would often prove invaluable in a life of ministry. Broughton wanted his faculty to be pastors and mentors, not simply lecturers and researchers. Yet he knew that such pastoring and mentoring occurred within the student body itself as an expression of other-centred care. This element is lost to theological education where time and space is not given to relationships.

Thorough yet Focussed

The fourth general aspect of Broughton's vision for theological education is his commitment to a thorough grounding in the word of God which remained in service to the ministry of that word in the Christian congregation and analogous groups. Broughton never played high academic standards off against a focus on gospel ministry in the churches. He consistently pursued the most thorough training possible. He extended the College course to four years — which he still thought should be considered a minimum! He longed to establish postgraduate work and a postgraduate community at the College. He encouraged the faculty to pursue the highest possible academic qualifications and to write as they had opportunity. He badgered the College Committee about the need to resource the Library so that it could support research at the Masters and Doctoral level. When students complained, as they did from time to time, about having to read and engage critical scholarship in biblical studies, he would insist upon how much there was to learn from such men, even though he found many of their assumptions unwarranted. Marcus Loane once summarised it this way: 'he set his heart on a highly qualified staff, on a wisely developed library, and on academic excellence'.[302] Yet this academic excellence was always in service of higher goals: the knowledge of God and 'training for the ministry'.

---

[302] Loane, *These Happy Warriors*, 59.

It was precisely because of the practical demands of gospel ministry that Broughton insisted on the highest possible academic standards. Practical ministry must be deeply theologically informed if it is not to descend into mere pragmatism or simple social activism. Conversely, every academic discipline needs to be integrated with 'prayer and the ministry of the word' (Acts 6.4). The fragmentation of the theological curriculum, so lamentably a characteristic of theological education around the world, was something Broughton Knox would not countenance. We return to his favourite biblical expression 'the whole counsel of God'. That is what effective practical ministry needed most.

But Broughton understood the lines to run in the other direction as well. Theological study, rigorously pursued, could not simply terminate with academic knowledge and be true to itself. What is learnt in the classroom necessarily pushes beyond the classroom into a life of fellowship with God and service of his people. Broughton once wrote that 'theology is an eminently practical science. Its purpose is to save and sanctify the soul'.[303] He was, of course, characteristically alluding to the words of Scripture: 'Therefore put away all filthiness and rampant wickedness and receive with meekness the implanted word, which is able to save your souls' (Jms 1.21). He could also have referenced Paul in his second letter to Timothy: '... the sacred writings, which are able to make you wise for salvation through faith in Jesus Christ' (2 Tim 3.15). God's revelation of himself is purposive. It shapes the life of those who receive it. It equips them for service (2 Tim 3.17) and it sets the contours of that service (1 Tim 4.6–16).

For these reasons, Broughton Knox would not have understood the modern attempt to categorise theological institutions as, on the one hand, those which are good at academic theology and, on the other, those which are good at practical ministry training. He would have refused the dichotomy. A true theology must not be isolated from the practice of ministry. A genuinely effective practice of ministry must be shaped and driven by the theology given to us in the Bible.

---

[303] D. B. Knox, 'Doctrine 1', Notes for the Preliminary Theological Certificate (Sydney: Moore College Committee for External Studies, c. 1966), 3.

The Enduring Legacy: The Modern Moore College

The Moore College of 2016 is very different from the college of 1985 let alone 1959 or 1947. So too is the context in which it operates and in which its graduates serve the churches. Operating within the higher education sector brings significant regulation and compliance issues that were unknown in Broughton's time. The Protestant ascendancy in which he was raised and which was still clearly demonstrable in his early years as Principal has faded, replaced at first by indifference and more recently by hostility. The expectations of new graduates of the College, whether their own or those of the senior minister or the congregation, are similarly different. The standard model of minister training throughout Broughton's time — four years in theological college followed by four years as a curate or assistant minister — has in many cases been replaced by a two-year apprenticeship followed by four years of theological education and so more is expected immediately upon graduation. The influence of England, English scholarship and models of ministry, has been challenged and in many places eclipsed by American evangelicalism, with its emphasis on size and pragmatism, and the power wielded by its publishing houses and Christian mega-conferences.

When Broughton Knox retired, there were 10 members of the full-time faculty and around 160 full-time students. Today the faculty numbers 20 with just under 300 full-time students, with part-time diploma students and post-grads as well. The Australian College of Theology's B.Th. was the standard degree taken in 1985, though the last of the London BD students were still preparing for their finals. Women attended Moore College lectures but were separately enrolled in Deaconess House. Today there are two women on the faculty, women are directly enrolled in the College, and the Priscilla and Aquila Centre has been established 'to benefit women and to encourage their ministries in partnership with men'.[304] The College's involvement with the Australian College of Theology's MTh program was still in its infancy, but now the College has its own MA and MTh as well as its own PhD. All these changes since Broughton's time and then the most obvious: when Broughton retired, the Broughton Knox Teaching Centre had not even been planned, let alone the new main campus building, which opened in February 2017.

---

[304] 'Our Mission', Priscilla and Aquila Centre website, https://paa.moore.edu.au.

Amid all these changes, the Knox priorities of faculty, library and residence remain. So too do the core values of the knowledge of God, the centrality of the Bible, the importance of relationships and high academic standards married to a consistent focus on other-centred word ministry. His dream of a robust postgraduate program has materialised while his commitment to lay theological education remains an important part of the College's mission. His legacy in terms of the physical plant of the College, but far more importantly, a coherent, deeply theological approach to the task of training men and women for the ministry shapes every facet of the modern Moore College. Few people in the current College ever had direct contact with Broughton Knox. Only three members of the current full-time faculty were ever taught by him (including the Principal) and we do have one of his grandchildren currently studying here. Yet every member of today's Moore College has great cause to thank God for what he did through this his servant during his long association with the College, and what he continues to do through his extraordinary and enduring legacy.

LEGACY 3: PEOPLE—PERSONAL REFLECTIONS AND EXPERIENCES

Paul Barnett

David Broughton Knox was one of the four people to whom I owe most gratitude, the others being Donald Robinson, Edwin Judge and Anita.

One is exceptionally blessed to have enjoyed the example and influence of people such as these.

In the case of Knox I had fourteen continuous years of almost daily contact with him. Four were as a student. Ten were as a faculty member of which during the last six I was also his rector (at St Barnabas, Broadway).

As part of the 1960's intake we were the second group to do the *four*-year course. We were an exceptionally large intake, the greatest to that point, due to the impact of the Graham Crusade the year before.

The establishment of the four-year course was one of Broughton's first initiatives as Principal. The four year long programme also provided the opportunity for some to engage the University of London BD, another of his key initiatives. The Preliminary Exam (five papers) fell half way through the second college year and the Finals (ten papers) in the middle of the fourth year.

Archbishop Gough was opposed to the four year programme but Knox stuck to his guns, and if I may be permitted a pun, argued to Gough that the four year course was like a long *gun* barrel. The longer the gun barrel the greater the exit velocity. Fourth year graduates would be shot further, for a longer period, and would be more effective ministers. Perhaps Broughton's time in the navy informed him about shipboard artillery. Who could be quick enough to answer Broughton's aphorisms?

On one occasion Gough mildly complained that college portraits of archbishops were hung too high. Quick as a flash Broughton observed that the college community liked to 'look up' to their archbishops.

I don't think their relationship proved to be a happy one.

Gough represented 'institution' and Broughton was no admirer of institution, especially since it was incarnated in an Englishman whose academic qualification was a 3rd in geography and whose theology was informed by campfire talks.

Baby boomer college students of the Vietnam generation loved the rebel in Broughton. I was a child of the depression so his gentle swipes at the diocese were a bit lost on me. One example was his reference to archdeacons who, he said, ran uselessly around the countryside grinning like dogs.

Broughton's vision for theological education was inspired by three goals: a well-educated faculty, extended undergraduate education, and an excellent library. That vision bore fruit in the number of Moore graduates who took higher degrees and who in turn became capable theological educators and writers.

At least two other colleges took their cue from Broughton: Trinity College in Perth founded by a college graduate Dr Allan Chapple (PhD Durham) and George Whitfield College in Capetown, founded by Broughton himself, and brilliantly developed by Dr David Seccombe, also a college graduate (PhD Cambridge).

It is testament to Broughton Knox that his successors as Principals at Moore College – Jensen, Woodhouse, and Thompson – have pursued his vision without, so far as I can see, altering its trajectory. In the years since, Moore College has been staffed by well-qualified academics, been blessed by a superb library and conducted exacting programmes for its students.

At the same time Broughton Knox did not pursue academic excellence for its own sake. It was all in the service of the gospel. Undergraduates were being trained for ministry and missionary service. The College's ongoing commitment to its annual missions is as Broughton would have wanted it.

For me, and for many, Broughton was a kind of father figure. Despite his sharp and penetrating wit he was essentially a man of gentle disposition. At the same time he summed up issues quickly with unerring accuracy that were expressed in a few well-chosen words. He was devastating in diocesan committees in the way he could just 'cut through' to the real point. Many if not all his students revered him. We felt that he cared about us and he was our guiding star.

Ailsa was a tireless, devoted and beautiful gospel yoke-fellow with Broughton. She greeted the stream of visitors to their home with friendship and grace, and was wonderfully hospitable. She was a great model of ministry hospitality whom Anita and I sought to emulate.

Broughton was a knowledgeable man. He had been schooled in Greek at the University of Sydney under – of all people – Enoch Powell. His Bible knowledge was exceptionable and he was at home with the early Fathers, and of course, with the Reformers – Calvin, Luther and Cranmer. Perhaps a weakness was a lack of engagement with current scholarship.

In class he did not impart much information as such, but rather *ideas*. These he communicated by making strong statements, even over-statements, at the beginning of classes that had the desired effect of provoking sometimes-outraged class outcry. But he would hold his ground so that by the end of the period we were all left thinking about what he said. I don't ever recall him being wrong, or at least admitting it.

But the thing is you would never pass an exam based on Broughton's input. Unlike today when lecturers bombard their classes with pages of notes and comprehensive lists of references with Broughton you came away with nothing, except ideas.

It was the same when Broughton ran tutorials in the early Fathers, my BD finals elective. He would throw out some ideas then climb up his little ladder and pull down something by Irenaeus or Athanasius. It was of little use in preparing for our exams. But that forced us to read, summarise and memorise various key textbooks.

But there was method in this apparent madness. If you wanted to pass or do well there was no alternative to doing extensive reading, summarising and memorising information from the best textbooks. I would have to say most of my knowledge came from what I have dug out from books and learned in such a way as to make the material my own. This wouldn't have happened if I had been spoon-fed.

Although not gifted with eloquence I regard Broughton Knox as a brilliant educator.

Broughton never seemed to be in a hurry. As a faculty member I was responsible for college fabric, which meant I often needed to raise matters of expenditure with the Principal. I would walk round the back of the chapel and as likely as not he would be sitting under a tree reading – his RSV Bible mostly. He wasn't overtly pious but in a deeper sense he was. He always had time and greeted me warmly. He was shrewd in money matters, and quick at arithmetic.

Broughton was a genius at acquiring property for the future development of Moore College, which he did in the face of strong opposition from diocesan officials and some members of the Standing Committee. He was savvy in money matters and somehow kept relentlessly buying old pubs and run down terrace houses. Such acquisitions today would be impossible given skyrocketing property prices.

Broughton had been attempting to get possession of one of the Carillon Avenue Houses and at last he succeeded. I will never forget the day we stood outside keys in hand. The inside of the house was nothing less than disgusting, but I will spare you the details. When I returned home to Anita she said, 'Hold still. There's a flea. There's another. Stand in the bath.' 'You'd better ring Ailsa', I said. She came back laughing. 'Ailsa said Broughton went straight to Standing Committee'.

I will be forever grateful that Broughton appointed me to his staff. I had been interviewed to work with Dudley Foord at Kingsgrove after ordination as a deacon, but somehow Broughton persuaded Gough that I should be ordained and work *under him* as his deacon. How he pulled that off I will never know. And so it came to pass that I did my curacy under D.B. Knox. I think I am the only one ever to have had that honour.

He indulged me by appointing me to teach early church history. Against the good-humoured ire of some faculty members Broughton allowed me to teach a whole, *two*-year course on the early Fathers (up to Chalcedon, 451). So my classes became very familiar with Stevenson's wonderful documents books, *A New Eusebius* and *Creeds, Councils, and Controversies*. Whatever the classes derived from those two years I do not know, but they were a huge boost for me. When I left the college I learned the faculty had rolled back my two-year Early Church History programme to one year.

Broughton insisted that I do arts subjects at Sydney University. This meant Classical Greek and Ancient History. In the latter I came under the spell of the Reader in Ancient History, Mr E. A. Judge, later the founding Professor of Ancient History at Macquarie University. I was later to teach in that department under his distinguished leadership.

Broughton's steering of me into classical studies set a new direction for me – as a journeyman historian, which I regard as the calling of God.

So, in short, I owe him a lot. More than I can say. I am confident that there would be dozens of others who could speak to his powerful influence in their lives.

In many ways Broughton was a shy man. He certainly didn't have much small talk. I think it was Peter O'Brien who was driving Broughton and F.F. Bruce somewhere. Bruce had no small talk either. I understand the driver almost crashed the car trying to get a conversation going.

But there was that wicked sense of humour that would pop up periodically. He once confided in me that sick motorcars get better. 'How so', I asked, exposing myself to the humour that I sensed was coming. 'Why', he said, 'last week I took the car for servicing, but couldn't afford the charges. This week I took it again and the list of repair items reduced. Obviously the remaining items were healed'.

One of Broughton's signature doctrines was that the NT word 'church' means a *local* gathering and not the denomination or institution. Initially I supported this view and indeed, wrote supporting it. Over the years I changed my mind a little on this. I concluded that he was right on what he affirmed but needed to be qualified in what he denied. I felt 'the people of God', or the example of the mission networks of Paul's churches, represented another reality alongside the autonomy of the local *ekklēsia* and that there were benefits for churches being part of an association of churches such as we have in the Diocese of Sydney. Community churches are not accountable. Sometimes local churches and/or their ministers fall out of line and need the discipline of the democratically elected diocesan leaders. In the matter of the Collection for the poor saints in Judea Paul calls on the church of Corinth to heed the leadership of brothers from the churches in Macedonia (2 Cor. 9:3-5). The church of Corinth was not autonomous but was to be subject to the admonitions of leaders from the Macedonian churches.

But apart from that my doctrinal position as shaped by Broughton Knox is unchanged. His moderate Calvinism (a four pointer), strong views on the authority of the Bible, the Trinitarian Godhead, Christology (he strongly argued for Christ's genuine humanity), and Atonement (strong on substitutionary atonement) have guided me in the intervening years.

In recent days I have been reflecting anew on the great reformers, Luther, Calvin and Cranmer. I have been thankful for the best in Luther and Calvin and feel that Cranmer picked those doctrines and emphases that *were* the best of Luther and the best of Calvin. I think Cranmer was *the* outstanding reformer who had the benefit of others going before him and I think that Broughton believed that too.

Broughton and his family were faithful members of St Barnabas Broadway. From time to time there were problems at the back of the church, for example, when a troubled woman charged a glass-fronted bookcase. Broughton always intervened helpfully, as he did on that occasion. He was a quiet encourager to the preacher, though he would point out any glitches. Once I had been preaching on the *Parable of the Wheat and the Tares* and wrongly identified the 'field' as the church. As Broughton left he just quietly said, 'the field is the world'.

I never stopped being surprised by Broughton. Once when the College team was engaged in a football match a player was knocked out. It was Broughton who rushed onto the field a secured the player's tongue and generally applied first aid. He gave the impression of being a bit vague and dreamy but you only had to see him swing into action to realize how wrong you were.

Glenn N. Davies

I had neither the honour nor the pleasure of being taught by Broughton Knox at Moore College. I was only enrolled in the Diploma of Arts in Theology, joining the fourth year cohort studying for the Bachelor of Divinity (London) in Moore College in 1980, and Broughton was on sabbatical for most of that year, so we only had a couple of lectures in fourth year on Canon Law. With the Principal on leave we had Donald Robinson for Canon Law for most of the lectures, and I recall in one memorable class that we were discussing lectionary readings. Bishop Robinson—he was Bishop in Parramatta at the time—was informing us of the importance of lectionary readings, their history and the mandatory nature of their being a part of Divine Service. One of the brave students in our class enquired of our lecturer: 'What if your Rector asks you to read a Bible reading relating to his sermon, which was not one of the lectionary readings?' Bishop Robinson replied, without humour: 'Then, you respectfully decline.'

At the end of the year Broughton came back from sabbatical and the same student (who will remain nameless) asked the Principal a similar question, while at the same time mischievously providing the answer that Bishop Robinson had given earlier in the year. Broughton replied without hesitation: 'Oh, the Bishop is quite mistaken. The obvious answer is that you read both!' That was quintessential Broughton: off the top of his head, he was able to answer a question with brevity, clarity and devastating effect.

My first encounter with Dr Knox was when I was at high school and he came to address our youth group. I remember being captivated by his breadth of knowledge and the way in which he quickly induced us to ask questions, whereupon I witnessed his wit and wisdom as he engaged his young audience.

The next opportunity I had to hear him, was when I was at Sydney University, in 1969. He spoke in the Stephen Roberts Lecture Theatre on the five points of Calvinism, expounding his views using Steele and

Thomas[305] as a foil for his own exposition of reformed doctrine, describing himself as a four-and-a-half point Calvinist. Within twelve months I had embraced the Reformed doctrines of grace and decided I wanted to go to College. I was in second year university, and I went and had an interview with Dr Knox. I was willing to leave university and enter College the following year, as I had been spurred on to learning more about God following my own epiphany concerning the authority of Scripture and God's sovereignty over all things. He wisely said: 'No, finish your university course. Go and get a job for a while—don't stay too long or the world will suck you in—and then study theology.' That was good advice and I acted on it. I finished university, went and got a job for a few years, and then pursued my theological education—alas, not at Moore College, but in the USA. I tried to meet with Broughton before I went overseas to study, but he was unfortunately away. However, I did meet with Dr Peter O'Brien, who sought to persuade me to come to Moore, but he was unsuccessful, so I went to Westminster Theological Seminary instead.

Upon completing my studies I returned to Sydney and entered fourth year at Moore College. I had a number of interviews with the Diocese with regard to ordination. There were all kinds of problems and I had many interviews—twenty-three, as I recall. I did not fit the mould for the ordination process. In one of my many meetings I met with Broughton, and he said: 'Oh, you've completed a four-year degree already, with a bachelor's degree and a master's degree, you don't need to do fourth year at College.' I said: 'Well, apparently, the Archbishop believes that I should come here to get some Anglican theology.' 'Anglican theology? Oh, I think the Archbishop is mistaken, we don't teach Anglican theology here. We teach what the Bible says!' Thus I entered into the world of Broughton Knox's thinking and his relationship with the Diocese. However, there was still some confusion as to whether or not I would need to undertake fourth year.

I later went and saw Archbishop Marcus Loane, and I said: 'I'm not sure whether the problem is actually at Moore College or in the Diocese.' Sir Marcus replied in that distinctive tone of voice (so often mimicked by clergy): 'I can assure you, the problem does not reside in the

---

[305] David N. Steele and Curtis C. Thomas, *The Five Points of Calvinism Defined, Defended and Documented* (Philadelphia: Presbyterian and Reformed, 1965).

Diocese!' I noticed then, perhaps for the first time, evidence of intriguing but differing opinions between these two brothers-in-law.

I was ordained in 1981 and spent two years in the parish of Willoughby. In May of my second year, I received a phone call from Broughton Knox who wanted to come and see me. I had no idea why he wanted to meet me. He drove to my house, and we had about half an hour's discussion inside. I didn't realize until later when I walked him back to his car that he had left his wife, Ailsa, in the car to wait until he had finished!

In our discussions he invited me to be a member of the faculty. I was surprised and astonished at this invitation as I had not contemplated being a lecturer at the time, and I naïvely declared: 'Dr Knox, I am not sure that I have any interest in joining the faculty.' He replied, with his usual aplomb: 'Oh, my dear brother, if you *wanted* to be a member of the faculty, we wouldn't ask you!' I said: 'But why me?' 'Oh, we've looked everywhere else!' He seemed to have an answer to every obstacle I put in his way, but I said I would think and pray about it.

I wasn't really quite sure, so I went and saw Dr Peter O'Brien again. Though he hadn't convinced me in our first conversation about coming to College, this time he was more successful in persuading me to join the faculty. His advice was to use the early years of my appointment to discern whether I could potentially be a long-time faculty member or if it were better to return to pastoral ministry, saying: 'You'll never know unless you actually dip your feet into the water, and you can always return to parish after a couple of years.'

So I did, and it was a wonderful experience. I was Broughton's last appointment on the faculty. I'd always called the Principal, 'Dr. Knox', and he invited me to call him Broughton, which was a big shift for a thirty-two year old. But that was very much an example of his ability to be personal; it was his doctrine of personal relationships put into practice. I saw that very much in his relationships with me and other members of the faculty. These were honoured, senior members of the faculty at the time, and I was obviously the junior member, but he (and they) treated me very much as their equal. I believe that Broughton's commitment to personal relationships and personal modes of address have been the catalyst for breaking down the barriers that existed between senior clergy and younger clergy in the Diocese. I actually have a book on the Lord's

Supper[306] that Broughton authored and dedicated to me personally. Well—it was dedicated to the faculty of Moore College, but that to me was a personal dedication, on the basis of Broughton's practice, seeing myself as being part of that illustrious company!

I was teaching biblical books in first year. Lecturing on 1 Timothy, the question of the extent of the atonement came up for discussion. I knew that Broughton had a different view to my own—I was a five-point Calvinist (and still am). One of my students said: 'Well, this is not what Dr. Knox says,' so I thought I'd better go and consult Broughton. We sat down in his garden outside the Principal's house, and I explained that I didn't want to be teaching something that was inconsistent with, let alone in opposition to, his own views on the subject, without his knowledge. Broughton's response to this young lecturer was ever so gracious. 'You must teach what the Bible says, and what you are convinced the Bible teaches. All I ask of you is that you be respectful of other people's views.' He did not start to expound his view, nor try to change my mind on the topic, nor give me the evidence against my position—which is something, I confess, I would have been tempted to do if I had been in his shoes. No, he let me teach what I believed the Bible to be saying. He had confidence in his faculty to teach the Bible faithfully. He believed that God would reveal to them the truth as they continued to submit to and learn from God's word, as they sought to expound it to others. I found that to be liberating as well as a remarkable piece of advice. This was not the immovable bronze statue of doctrinal orthodoxy, with cold and clinical precision destroying others' views without feeling or compassion, which some critics of Broughton would contend. This was the thoughtful, wise and pastorally sensitive Broughton, seeking to minster to those under his care.

There are lots of interesting anecdotes that could be told, as there are lots of questions that I wish I'd asked Broughton during those treasured years on his faculty. During morning tea in the faculty common room—the annex off the Moore College Dining Hall—there would often be questions posed and views exchanged which were regularly, intellectually stimulating. I remember, on one occasion, we were talking about the application of the Ten Commandments for today. If I'm not mistaken, Robert Doyle said that he only considered nine out of ten to be relevant to Christians, because the Sabbath was no longer required under

---

[306] Knox, *Lord's Supper from Wycliffe to Cranmer.*

the new covenant. Broughton dryly replied: 'Oh, if I were going to drop one of the Ten Commandments, it wouldn't be the fourth!' Silence descended. No one had the courage to ask which one he would have dropped! That's a regret I still carry to this very day.

When Peter Jensen was announced as the new Principal, he appointed me as the Registrar. Broughton didn't complete his term as Principal until the end of February 1985, and as Registrar I had organized the inaugural registration day. Such an event was unknown in the annals of Moore College: to know what classes you were going to attend and where they'd be held, and for faculty to have a list of students in advance for each of their classes was a complete novelty! Broughton came into the room and loudly exclaimed: 'Oh, this is wonderful—and it has happened while I've been Principal!' That too was classic Broughton.

I'll never forget another occasion, on a Tuesday night in the Upper T. C. Hammond Common Room where we gathered for chapel before the evening meal. As Registrar, I knew who was on duty for preaching that night—it was one of the faculty members. The time came for the sermon, and the student who was leading the chapel waited for the appointed person to preach—obviously the student hadn't checked who was rostered. There was a deathly silence. Nothing happened; no one got up. So Broughton jumped up, and said, 'No problem, I'll preach!' He then began to deliver an extempore sermon, on the faithfulness of Christ (*pistis christou*), and it was, in my view, one of the best sermons I ever heard Broughton preach. Off the cuff, he went through the various texts, and gave a well ordered, systematic and convincing argument for reading the phrase as a subjective genitive and its importance and application to us as Christians. There was Broughton at his best: using all the gifts and skills that God had given him to bring forth the word of God in a way which was both memorable and extraordinary.

When I became a member of the faculty, I said I was not interested in pursuing a higher degree. Broughton had said at the time of my appointment: 'No, you've got a master's degree, that's all right.' Then about six months later, he said: 'Have you thought about doing a Ph.D.?' I said: 'No. You remember our conversation don't you?' 'Oh, well I've just put an application in for a scholarship to study overseas, so you can gain a Ph.D.!' I said: 'Really? How can you apply on my behalf?' Little did I realise that the Principal of Moore College and the Rector of St Thomas'

North Sydney were the ones who awarded this particular scholarship.[307] It just so happened that I was attending St Thomas' North Sydney in my first year on the faculty as a Sunday curate. Strangely enough, I won the scholarship and so went to the UK to engage in doctoral studies.

When I came back, Broughton had left and moved to South Africa to establish the George Whitfield College,[308] but he returned to Sydney in the early nineties. It was in late 1993 that Broughton and I had our last two conversations.

The first was prior to the marriage of Michael Hill, who was engaged to my Deputy Registrar, Wendy Dahl, and they'd invited me to preach the sermon at their wedding. I remember talking to Broughton and saying, 'I've got this sermon to preach. There'll be more Revs than at a Bathurst car rally attending this wedding! What am I going to preach on?' Broughton said with his usual sagacity, 'Just preach the gospel, that's what you do! That's what Michael and Wendy need: preach the gospel!'

My last conversation with Broughton was at the wedding reception. While I had followed nearly all of Broughton's advice up to this point of time, in the providence of God, his final piece of advice was overruled. Our final conversation ended with these salutary words from Broughton: 'Stay at the College, theological education is too important to do anything else—and don't become a bishop!'

---

[307] The Joan Augusta MacKenzie Travelling Scholarship.

[308] George Whitfield College is an Anglican evangelical theological college in Muizenberg, Cape Town, South Africa, where D. B. Knox was the College's founding Principal.

Graeme Goldsworthy

My first encounter with DBK came a while before I entered Moore College. It may not be a surprise to many that the issue was the sovereignty of God. I was a student at Sydney University and, one lunch time, a group of us from the EU were eating together on the front lawn. The subject of capital punishment came up and one of our number, with clearly Arminian views, proposed that the death penalty was not appropriate because, 'while there's life there's hope that the condemned will hear the gospel and be saved.' Another in the group, obviously a Calvinist, responded with what, to me then, was an extraordinary suggestion. He said, 'If that man is predestined to eternal life, he will be converted before he is executed.' This was new territory for me for I suppose I was at that time by nature a pietistic Arminian. My brother John was studying at Moore College, so at the first opportunity I asked him what he thought. He grabbed some lecture notes, gave them to me, and said, 'Read what Broughton has to say about it.' Of course the hearsay evidence of a student's lecture notes was not necessarily entirely accurate, but nevertheless it blew my mind to have the matter of God's sovereignty opened up to this degree in Broughton's inimitable way. Thus, when I entered college a year or two later, I had already been instructed by Broughton in an important way.

When I started the two years of Th. L. studies in 1956, Broughton was Vice-Principal and had taken over lecturing in Christian Doctrine from the recently retired T. C. Hammond. I consider myself fortunate to have had Donald Robinson for Old Testament, Marcus Loane for New Testament, and Broughton for Doctrine. All of them had an enormous impact on my life and thought. Over the years since then, I have mislaid, lost, or simply got rid of notes I took in lectures. But, I made sure I kept the notes I took in Broughton's lectures, and they are still with me.

I have been privileged to sit at the feet of a number of great biblical scholars. When I left Moore, I had a B. A. degree from Sydney University and a B. D. from the University of London, and the Th. L. diploma of the Australian College of Theology. Even after a further two years at Cambridge, and then later three years at Union Presbyterian Seminary in Richmond, Virginia, I said then, and have continued to say until this day, that Broughton's Doctrine lectures where the highlight of my academic experience. I have thought much about why this is. The following reasons spring to mind, although no description can really recapture the ethos of a Broughton lecture!

First, he was ruthlessly biblical. That meant, among other things that, apart from the Greek and Hebrew, one should use the 1881-85 English Revised Version. Hence, this response after a student quoted the KJV to oppose something Broughton had said: 'If you want to quote the Bible, you must *have* the Bible!' More importantly it meant that we went where the Bible took us, and that we were not foreordained to follow any particular denominational or academic tradition.

Second, as well as the usual run of Sydney Anglican Pietists, our class included several Anglo-Catholics, at least one Thompson Chain Reference KJV devotee, and even the odd Dispensationalist or two. When questioned, Broughton would always rise to the occasion and get a really lively debate going. Lectures were rarely uninteresting because of the cut and thrust of animated, but good natured, theological debate.

Third, although the subject named 'Doctrine' implied Church Dogmatics or Systematic Theology, Broughton's style was to aim at a more integrated approach in which the three major disciplines of Biblical, Systematic, and Historical Theology were all considered. At times I found the history of, for example, the Christological debates somewhat rarefied, but eventually came to realise how important it was to have some grounding in the theology of the Fathers. Broughton was more interested in the Fathers and the Reformers than in the modern theologians whom he largely ignored.

Fourth, I found Broughton's emphasis on Reformed Theology irresistible. We were required to read through Calvin's Institutes during the two Th.L. years. I was not the only one at the time who thought this a bit of an imposition. But, what better way to get a grasp on Reformed Theology without resorting to a rigid and pedestrian treatment of the Five Points. Broughton's integrated approach meant examining the biblical theology of grace along with the patristic writings before looking at the systematic theology of the Reformation.

After my two years pursuing the Tripos Part III in Cambridge, and a year with the Episcopal Church in the Diocese of New York, I was invited by Broughton to join the Moore College faculty to lecture Old Testament and Hebrew. I held this position from the start of the academic year in 1963 until I and my family left for the USA in August 1969. Serving under Broughton's principalship was a formative time for me. As I remember it, it was largely during this period that Broughton broke the mould that had long existed at Moore. Students who could qualify were encouraged to study for the London B.D. A part-time fourth year for recent graduates was introduced to enable them to start on the Th. Schol. Diploma. This replaced the deacon's year that had consisted of lectures on Friday mornings. The course structure for students of Deaconess House also underwent some changes. I found myself lecturing to a Deaconness Diploma class in what was really Biblical Theology. The academic expansion of the college was largely due to Broughton's foresight.

Broughton clearly saw his time as Principal as the opportunity to expand the infrastructure of the campus. This was largely a matter of purchasing adjacent properties whenever possible. For some of us on the faculty it meant that our housing was not a priority. This influenced my decision to grasp the opportunity to go to the USA in 1969 for graduate studies. However, I came to look back on this time, difficult though it was for some members of faculty, as one characterized by Broughton's dogged determination to expand the campus as well as the academic standing of Moore. There was need for a campus in which increasing numbers of students could be accommodated and taught by a growing faculty, in adequate lecture rooms, and with access to a library that was able to grow under Broughton's leadership into a formidable undergraduate and graduate library. When Donald Robinson left the faculty to become Bishop in Parramatta, I was just returning from the USA. At the end of 1972, there being no vacancy on the college faculty, I took up the parish of Yagoona. Broughton invited me to come in one morning a week to lecture the first-year course in Biblical Theology. This had been Don Robinson's domain since its inception in the 1950's. It was this experience that led to my writing *Gospel and Kingdom*, which was based on the Robinsonian structure of the course I developed.

After twenty years in Brisbane I returned to the Moore Faculty in 1995. The changes since the 60's were immense and, in my opinion, largely due to the momentum of change that Broughton had achieved. The changes were to be seen, first, in the consolidation of the campus to be more family-friendly and student-oriented. Second, the enlarged faculty in which there was an increase in the academic qualifications, but never at the expense of spiritual maturity and leadership. Third, there was the academic accreditation that has been achieved along with Moore's right to give its own degrees. Fourth, we give thanks for the growth of the library into the magnificent collection that it now is for both undergraduate and graduate study. Fifth, from being a Sydney Diocesan college for Anglican ordinands, Moore had become more inter-denominational and international. Sixth, the diocesan external studies courses, which began under T. C. Hammond, and were encouraged by Broughton, have become a world-wide ministry. I cannot think of any aspect of the present achievements of the college that, under God and by his grace, does not owe much to the foresight and strategic planning of David Broughton Knox. But, as I sure he would acknowledge, he stood on the broad shoulders of many who went before him, and on the formative events stretching back to Richard Johnson's arrival with the First Fleet in 1788.

Graham Cole

I first sighted and heard Dr Knox (DBK) speak in 1969 at the University of Sydney. Hundreds were there listening to the white haired figure down the front. He gave five lectures on the five points of Calvinism. One point each week. The style was unadorned and the voice idiosyncratic. The subject matter was compelling as I listened as a new Christian to the lectures filled with Scripture quotations. Next to my conversion to Christ in 1967, those five weeks were the most transformative experience in my life. Though these days I lean towards an Amyraldian-like Calvinism much like DBK's own.

Moore College soon beckoned and so there I was sitting in the Principal's residence in 1971 inquiring about admission the very next year. DBK was pastorally sage. He found out that I was newly married and suggested I wait a year longer which I did. How right he was. Doctrine 1 was an education as long as someone in the class asked a question or two. Thankfully that happened nearly every week. Questions galvanized DBK. Otherwise class could be deadly. One memorable class began with DBK beginning to give the lecture he had given the week before. A student pointed the problem out. 'Oh,' DBK said, 'You cannot hear the truth too often.' So he gave the same lecture all over again.

I joined the full time Moore faculty in 1980 and DBK became my MTH supervisor. I did a thesis on Thomas Cranmer's theology of the Bible and the godly prince. We had many an enjoyable supervisory session and on occasion about Cranmer. I came to appreciate that DBK was not fond of yes people. I had disagreed with him at times as a student and then as a faculty member. However, disagreement was always at the level of ideas never personal. On many, many occasions I experienced his kindness.

DBK could be blunt. I recall in my University of Sydney student days his giving a lecture on Roman Catholicism. A Roman Catholic student took issue with him over Vatican II. DBK responded, 'You have never heard the truth [that Catholicism was still officially Tridentine, despite Vatican II] put so plainly to you.' I felt the mood of the lecture hall change in an instant at that point. DBK had largely lost the audience. He also ran an argument at times that women should not preach because of the weakness of their voice boxes. I wondered if he had ever heard Dame Judi Dench play Queen Elizabeth 1.

He could also be very funny in a wry way. There were two Drs Knox in Carillon Avenue: Principal Knox and his brother, the gynaecologist. In my last year as a theological student, my wife was pregnant with our first child and there on our fridge in Little Queen Street was a letter addressed to Dr Knox. I grabbed it and put it in Principal Knox's mail slot. Soon I was summoned to the Principal's residence. At the door I was handed back the now opened envelop with its intimate details. DBK said that he thought it was for his brother. He then added: 'I could do the job, but I cannot guarantee the workmanship.' I realized my mistake and red faced retreated in haste. He could also be quaint. I was so pleased that when I turned forty he stopped calling me, 'Dear boy.'

In 1992 I left Moore College after many happy years there and became the Principal of Ridley College in Melbourne. A letter from DBK soon came. He knew the strategic importance of Ridley as it is independent of any diocese even though it is Anglican. I was so green. Any advice was most welcome. The message was plain. Faculty is the key to the success under God of any theological college. Pick the best and that meant more than simply academically best. This was wise advice never to be forgotten.

Over the years of our fellowship I learned so much from DBK. Not the least I learned to be an independent thinker if I believed I had biblical warrant to be such on an issue. DBK was so comfortable in his theological skin that he could respond to a different idea or challenge rather than be merely reactive. I so appreciated that non-anxious leadership. The importance of the doctrines of the Trinity and of the church, a high view of Scripture, the gracious nature of the gospel, the value of prayer have all stayed with me. His emphasis on fellowship between persons starting with the Holy trinity led me to ask the transcendental question: What else must be true if this view of relationships is true? This in turn led me to develop a personalist metaphysic, epistemology and axiology. No one has influenced me more theologically than Broughton.

D. A. Carson

My wife and I spent the (northern hemisphere) academic year 1980-81 at Tyndale House, Cambridge. We had been there five or six months when, in January 1981, Broughton and Ailsa Knox arrived from Australia, and moved into the flat above us. I knew he was Principal of Moore Theological College, but that's about all I knew of him. We briefly conversed two or three times at elevenses and during afternoon tea. Somewhere toward the end of the month, Broughton and Ailsa invited Joy and me up to their flat for Sunday tea.

We had barely sat down, when Broughton asked – more, it seemed to me, by way of accusation than inquiry – 'You're a Baptist minister, aren't you?'

I pleaded guilty. Broughton set the agenda by declaring, 'Of course, there is no such thing as baptism in the New Testament.'

After a couple of exchanges, he qualified this by saying there was little or no emphasis on water baptism. All the emphasis lay on Spirit baptism. I responded that such a restriction was going to make the interpretation of Mark 1:10 a little difficult, where Jesus at his baptism is said to come out of the water.

And so it went for two hours. Again and again I tried to turn the conversation to other topics. I asked Ailsa how many children she had, and what they were doing. Broughton was relentless. Invariably he returned to his own agenda. Ailsa sat there, very prim and proper, offering little unless Joy or I managed to put a question to her. My wife Joy watched the back-and-forth with the neck rotation one normally associates with people who are watching a tennis match. After two hours, we managed to make our escape. On the way down the stairs, Joy pronounced, 'That is the rudest man I have ever met!'

A few weeks later I received a warm letter from Broughton Knox, inviting me to deliver the Moore College lectures in 1985, on any mutually agreed subject. Apparently I had passed the test. Only later, as I came to know him better, both on his own and through the eyes of his students, did I learn how quintessentially Broughton that afternoon had been: very little place for small talk, much theological argument, pushing his students in a way that required them to push back, Socratic methods, independent thinking. I soon learned that most of his many students came to revere him; a minority came to loathe him. Almost no one was neutral about him.

Some years later, over the course of a week I preached through the Johannine Epistles at one of the Katoomba conferences. Broughton Knox attended. After most of the sermons, he said nothing much at all, and certainly nothing positive. Then came the day I preached through 1 John 5. The apostle John spends much of his focus in this chapter showing how the three so-called 'tests of life' (the expression comes from Robert Law) are tangled up together. There are not really three separate tests; rather, they are so intertwined that they stand or fall together. It's not 'best two out of three' or anything like that. One is either a Christian, or one is not, John is telling us, and this is what Christians look like, over against the opponents: they affirm central gospel truths, they gladly bow to the Lordship of Jesus, and they love one another – and these three descriptors are intrinsically tightly interwoven so that you cannot truly display any one of them without displaying the other two. Broughton rushed up to me after the sermon and declared, 'Now that's preaching!'

Once again, as I got to know the man better, I better appreciated his criteria. In some ways, Broughton was a big-picture thinker; more importantly, he loved integration, how the individual pieces of the Bible needed to be understood together. From my perspective, I brought things together in that sermon because the text I was expounding brought things together; I had done less integration in earlier passages of 1 John because as far as I could see John himself had done less of it – and there is a case for letting the high point of a series of sermons arrive toward the end of the series. But for Broughton, good preaching must include careful integration. I'm not sure he was wrong.

My last vignette of Broughton is also connected with Katoomba, where, once again, I was preaching at some conference or other. Broughton and Ailsa, along with their in-laws, Marcus Loane and his wife, invited me to lunch at the Blue Mountains cottage of the Loanes. The five of us – the Loanes, the Knoxes, and I – sat down to a lovely lunch with brisk conversation on many things. It was not long before the topic of conversation turned to the 1959 Billy Graham Australia Crusade – that remarkable series of meetings in which many thousands of people were genuinely converted. From this pool of converts sprang up many of Australia's most influential Christian leaders of the next generation. I had heard some of the stories, and had read one or two books on that 1959 Crusade, but now I had eyewitnesses seated at the same table. I asked questions, and the stories flowed: the meetings and the conversions that flowed from them had characteristics commonly associated with genuine revival. I wish I had had a tape-recorder running. The accounts were candid, mesmerizing, wonderful – glorious reminders of what God can do when he lays bare his arm in surprising gospel power.

About 3:00 or 3:30 pm, Broughton drove me back up to the Speaker's Lodge. (I cannot forbear to mention that 'Speaker's Lodge' is in this context a magnificent euphemism.) We sat in his car for an hour and a half, talking mostly about the doctrine of God. He wanted to write a book on the topic. As we chatted, two things became obvious, both of them typical of Broughton: he had a deep, reverent, independent turn of mind that forged uncommon but insightful connections, while his knowledge of secondary literature was deep with respect to a handful of authors of whom he thought highly, and oblivious to the rest. I could not help thinking that if one has to choose between a teacher with a deep knowledge of Scripture but a slim grasp of the secondary literature, and a teacher with a slim knowledge of Scripture but a voluminous grasp of the secondary literature, I know which one I'd prefer. And I have little doubt which of these two teachers is likely to reflect more of the mind of God.

Between 5:00 and 5:30 pm, I excused myself and left his car. He drove home to his own cottage. At about 6:30 he suffered a massive stroke. He never regained consciousness. Several weeks later he slipped into eternity. So his last day on earth in full possession of his faculties, he spent talking about the 1959 Billy Graham meetings which uniquely displayed revival-like characteristics, and about the doctrine of God.

I can think of worse ways to end one's life.

APPENDICES

The Challenge of Writing Broughton Knox's Biography

Marcia Cameron

It's not easy now to remember how hard that mountain was to climb. Even as you gain the summit, somehow, looking down, back to where you toiled up the slopes, they no longer seem steep, and neither does the path seem long. But in prospect, climbing that mountain was almost beyond me. So high, so far away, so steep, so perilous. It has always been the case, whether it was working on my Master's thesis, or later on a PhD. And very much so with the biography of Broughton Knox.

To change the imagery: as I began the task, I felt like a craft setting off for a known destination. But how I would get there, what would happen, and what adventures would overtake me, were all part of the voyage. I intended to reach port, but there were times when I wondered if I would.

I had never written a biography before, but had long wanted to, inspired years ago by J Pollock's biographies of famous Christians. So, of course, one challenge was, simply, would I have the requisite skill?

Broughton Knox is a marvellous subject for a biographer. An evangelical guru, a highly intelligent man, a godly man, one with an unusually flexible mind, one who was shy and reserved, who inspired strong reactions, both positive and negative. Colourful, complex and enigmatic. I had been searching in my mind for a subject, and had come up with nothing. I discussed the 'who?' question with my husband Neil, and he suggested Broughton Knox. It was an excellent suggestion, since I had had some contact with Broughton over the years, and was inspired by the thought of him as my subject.

We all have a bias, and it is important for the author to recognize what his or her bias is. This is the 'given' for writing any kind of history these days. Whatever mine was would affect the way I told Broughton's story, the way I perceived information about him, and my evaluation of material from lots of interviews. I wanted to end up being truthful about Broughton, but also kind. I wanted to be accurate and also balanced.

THE CHALLENGE OF WRITING BROUGHTON KNOX'S BIOGRAPHY

It is a fine tight-rope to walk: to state the truth as one perceives it, and in an appropriate way. On a number of occasions I relied on the discerning reader to join the dots if they were to understand what I wanted to communicate. By the time I came to write Broughton's biography, I had had some practice in the art of choosing the best word available. There is a range of words in our marvellous language for many concepts: some bald and bold, some more subtle and nuanced. Years of reading CS Lewis and other masters of the English language had, without question, helped.

Those biographers whose subject is either still alive or who has living relatives has a major challenge. For me it was the most significant challenge. One can write more freely about someone who died 50 years ago. In my case Alisa, Broughton's wife, still lived, and there were his children to consider as well. I discussed Broughton with Ailsa over many interviews, and I gave her my draft MS for comment. I tried, in other words, to be transparent as to what I intended to publish, and I tried to understand her point of view and modify what I written, where possible. I don't think she liked the published biography, although she was too gracious to say so. One of Broughton's children didn't read the biography for years. But one afternoon I found a note on my doorstep, thanking me for it, and stating that everything in the book that that child knew about, was accurate. It was a great moment for me.

Some of Broughton's adult children and relatives consented to be interviewed. Some did not want to be referenced in the footnotes as sources. There were one or two people whose view of Broughton Knox was such that they refused to be interviewed and told me why.

Memory is notoriously unreliable, so I had to ensure that claims emerging from an interview could be substantiated. There were some claims that I was inclined to believe, but because they could not be cross-checked, I could not in all honesty include them. There was some marvellous material in the interviews which I would love to have included. But because it was tangential to the biography and would upset some readers, I ended up not using it.

As the biographer of a Christian leader, while I certainly did not want to write a hagiography, I did not want to air dirty washing. Hagiography is a form of falsehood, and most unhelpful for Christians battling along on life's journey. And dirty washing aired just for its own sake, while sometimes fascinating, is quite unhelpful for the gospel. It is simply bad press for the Christian faith, and especially unhelpful to those outside the Christian fold.

In terms of research, I found the writing project a huge one. Broughton's life was painted on a very large canvas, so there was a great deal to research and understand. There was the family's Irish and English background, early days in Queensland and Kangaloon, wartime England, Broughton's naval years, the complexities of the Diocese of Sydney, and South Africa. The development of Broughton's theology, and evaluating his published works, his radio talks and his Oxford DPhil, were challenges to one who is an historian, not a formally trained theologian. One of the great benefits of writing about Broughton was the huge amount I learned, both in interviews and through research.

The most important challenge was to understand how Broughton Knox ticked. Some biographies leave one no better informed about their subject than before one read them, as the character never really comes alive. Instead the background events and characters take over, and result is like an opera singer who is outmusiked by the orchestra. It is essential for a biographer to have a genuine interest in people, how they think, how they relate, what drives them, and how they came to be the way they are. I had always found Broughton Knox fascinating, so that, I suppose, was a good start. We had quite a few meals with him and Ailsa, over the years. I discovered early on that a good way to put him at ease and hear him at his best was to ask him a question. As I asked it, I mentally visualized myself turning on a garden tap. That way I learned a lot about him and his ideas. Presumably other people did the same.

Talking with Ailsa, with Broughton's sisters and with his children, not to mention former staff and students at both Moore College and George Whitefield College, gave me insights into his complex personality. One thing I particularly admire about him was his *flexibility*: while holding onto the fundamentals, he was willing to examine ideas, think creatively and even change his mind. This was at times hugely frustrating for those who had to work with him. For the head of an august diocesan institution for a quarter of a century, he was, I think, amazingly non-institutionalised. It was indeed a challenge to get right the balance of the contradictions which lay within his personality, and neither to idealise nor belittle him.

THE CHALLENGE OF WRITING BROUGHTON KNOX'S BIOGRAPHY

Broughton Knox stirred up exaggerated responses. Some loved and revered him as their father in God: others detested him. There were many who respected and loved him. In others, he stirred up all those reactions. Working out the extent to which he was, and continues to be, a major influence in the Diocese of Sydney is a challenge. Today's symposium which is exclusively focussed upon David Broughton Knox, in the year of his centenary, speaks for itself. Has such a thing ever happened before in this Diocese? The Diocese of Sydney is certainly a phenomenon, and it might be said that this is due to David Broughton Knox, more than to any other single leader.

There was a point at which I wondered whether the biography would be published. From early on I had a publisher, Acorn Press, in Melbourne, and I had nothing but support from them for my work. I cannot remember the details of my difficulties, but they were certainly serious. One major problem related to what material should or should not be included. A bishop's wife in Melbourne, knowing something of my plight, as her husband was the Chairman of Acorn Press, told me that in her opinion I was being bullied. I was sustained in those difficult months by Broughton Knox's brother-in-law, Archbishop Sir Marcus Loane. Having evinced a strong interest in the biography's progress, he avidly read each new chapter of the MS when I delivered it to him, despite his failing eyesight. Then we would have a subsequent discussion. His advice to me was: 'Don't change a word!' When the time came for the book launch at Moore College, as the keynote speaker he gave a brilliant speech, without notes.

Acorn Press required a contribution of $10,000 towards the costs. I am indebted to Dr Robert Tong, Sir Marcus' son-in-law and a member of the Moore College Council, who managed to persuade the Council to underwrite the book for that amount.

The final challenge was to see the book published in time for the launch. It arrived at the College in its cardboard boxes on the actual day of the launch. I first took up a copy in my hands an hour before the launch began.

Broughton Knox: Some Fragments and Reminiscences

Robert Tong

A Caveat

While there are footnotes and references, this is not a scholarly paper. There is no deep question to examine. If there is any coherence to this contribution it lies in the title: 'some fragments and reminiscences' with perhaps a subconscious theme of Broughton's interface with the world beyond Sydney.[309]

Argument and Debate

Argument and debate was meat and drink to Broughton from a young age. Marcia Cameron, describing a time when Broughton was still at school, puts it like this:

> There were many verbal battles around the dining table when Broughton, the most skilled in his use of words, would demolish his opponents.[310]

Family oral history bears out this contention.[311] His skills in argument and debate were finely honed during his two years (1942-3) at Cambridge.[312] This intense inter- personal teaching method put one's intellectual metal under the hammer. You will pick up the intensity of the Cambridge tutorial[313] system of instruction from this extract from a recent history faculty newsletter.

> The unique strengths of the undergraduate education in History are obvious. As soon as students arrive, they are

---

[309] I acknowledge a significant debt to Marcia Cameron's biography (Cameron, *Enigmatic Life*.) for it provided much background information for this paper.
[310] Ibid., 35.
[311] My mother in law was Patricia Loane and Broughton was her brother. On my marriage to Winsome Loane 'Mr Knox' became 'Uncle Broughton'.
[312] Fitzwilliam College.
[313] A similar method of instruction is found at Oxford where the 'supervisions' are called 'tutorials'.

thrown into the deep end, assigned reading from the frontiers of historical debate, and told to digest it in the form of a weekly essay. This challenge is mitigated by lectures and especially by the supervision (still most often one-on-one) where students are coached in a highly personal way. At the end of the first two years, students face a battery of five three-hour exams. The Part I exams are a test of capacity and discipline certifying that students are ready not just for Part II but for all kinds of futures beyond graduation. It's an extraordinary education![314]

Those here today who experienced Broughton's doctrine lectures can attest to his enjoyment and preference for dealing with a student's question over delivering a straight lecture. Hitler's war intervened before Broughton could complete the requirements for the degree and at the age of 28 he joined the Royal Navy Volunteer Reserve as a chaplain.[315]

A Snippet from the War Diary.[316]

On Tuesday (D Day 6 June 1944) news came over the wireless that the attack had begun. Everybody was pleased. The relief was inexpressible. Early next morning the Cap Tourane left Southend and steamed towards Dover. We were in a large convoy. A number of small escort vessels circled around. Our speed was only eight knots so we lost position by the time we reached the straits we were second last. The ships in front had put up strong smoke screens and had got through unmolested. But by the time we arrived the Germans had sighted the convoy and had opened fire. They fired six Salvoes at us. Some of them were unpleasantly close, falling just a little forward and just a little aft of the ship. Those who saw them fall estimated that the nearest was from 15 to 30 yards away.

---

[314] Cambridge History Faculty Newsletter, August 2016. Broughton took the Part l exams in divinity but did not proceed to Part ll because he joined the war effort.
[315] Royal Navy chaplains were commissioned by the Sovereign but held no military rank, unlike the RAF where Chaplain Stuart Barton-Babbage had the rank of squadron leader and in the Australian army where Chaplain Marcus Loane was a captain.
[316] Next quotations taken from a typed version of 'Dr Knox' Diary' presently in the possession of the writer.

Several times the ship was plastered with shrapnel. When action stations was sounded I went to the sick bay and chatted with the first aid party. Later I went onto the mess deck to talk to the Marines. Our ship was very fortunate not to be hit. It was an unpleasant feeling to know that we were the target of heavy guns who had got our range fairly accurately. And that we had only eight knots. However, the only casualty was a gunner slightly grazed with shrapnel. There were no further incidents that day.

The opportunities for spiritual work on board this ship have so far been very wonderful. We hold a Bible study group in the ship's office twice a week. A mid-week hymn singing was well attended. People are very ready to listen to direct spiritual talks and I find that I am more able to speak directly.

Monday (12 June): yesterday was distinguished only by a desultory naval bombardment. Learned that Maurice Wood[317] was ashore and was working very hard. Asked the Commander's permission to go ashore to help him but afterwards had an attack of the jitters, as the beach was still being shelled and snipers were reported to be active - French women were joining their ranks. This attack was the result of lack of prayer and meditation.

I left the ship in LCVP[318] and near the shore transferred to a DUKW[319]. Running up the shore was a time for

---

[317] The Rev Maurice Ponsonby Wood MA (Cantab), Royal Marine Chaplain, landed with a Royal Navy Beach Commando on D Day and the next day he found a portable organ and on a French beach and claimed to have held the first Anglican service on French soil after the landings. In July of that year he joined the 48 Royal Marine Commando and swam ashore with his unit in the assault at Walcheren and accompanied them as far as the Rhine. He was awarded the Distinguished Service Cross. After the war, he became successively, Rector of St Ebbe's Oxford, Vicar St Mary's Islington (in his time a leading centre for Evangelical leadership), Principal, Oak Hill College, and finally in 1971 Bishop of Norwich. A distinguished evangelical leader, a friend of Sydney diocese and he never wore a mitre!

[318] Landing Craft Vehicles Personnel.

[319] Amphibious vehicle used to land troops and equipment.

holding one's breath, as some of the mines had not been removed. Met Wood who is living in a German dug out. The Germans had certainly built a very intricate series of strong points, connected by underground passages. There were a number of German prisoners working on the beach. I took a lorry drive inland to the war cemetery. It was a most interesting trip, passing gun sights and impediments of war on every hand. The countryside is very pretty. The cemetery is an orchard, a field surrounded by giant trees and overlooked by a Norman church tower. We had a short sermon at the graveside. It was a moving scene as we prayed over the bodies of the men who had died. We had lunch with Wood and a couple of other Naval chaplains and two doctors on the beach. Underneath the sand on which we were sitting was a German dug out. A strange place for a picnic! After lunch I returned to the ship in a DUKW. No enemy activity on the beach while I was ashore. I was never less than one and a half miles from enemy held territory during my peregrinations!

Tyndale House

When one walks into the sitting room of Tyndale House Cambridge, there on a bookshelf is a framed, black and white photograph of Broughton. It is there because he was a prime mover in the establishment of that research library. T A Noble tells us:

> Following the Kingham Hill conference, FF Bruce was invited to join the Biblical Research Committee and during 1942 he was asked to succeed GT Manley in the chair. At a conference of the committee held at 37 Trinity Street Cambridge during the IVF Leaders' Conference from 7 to 10 September 1942, Manley 'called vigorously for young men to act. Bruce became chairman and Stuart Barton Babbage, now an RAF chaplain with the rank of squadron leader, succeeded John Wenham as secretary. *Of all the business transacted at this significant meeting, none was of greater significance for the future than WJ Martin's presentation of a report written by Broughton Knox (also now on the committee but abroad for two*

> *years) to advocate their joint proposal for a residential research library.* (emphasis added)[320]

The Martin-Knox proposal was for a large house for a library, small conferences and accommodation for research scholars.

> It would provide *a headquarters for the co-ordination, and direction, of Conservative Evangelical biblical scholarship...*the primary object should be constantly emphasised and preserved, that is, to make the library a research centre and that it should maintain a high standard in all publications which may be issued from it and in any study courses which should be organised. All other functions should be strictly subservient to this primary aim. (emphasis added)[321]

Do we see the present and future shape of Moore College in these terms? In Broughton's mind 'library and faculty' were the essential building blocks for a theological college, echoes of Tyndale House?

Library

In 1961 Noel Pollard[322] joined the Moore College faculty and carried the title of 'Librarian'. In a 1994 letter to Ailsa Knox[323] he wrote:

> Then my memory of Broughton goes back to those frequent conversations that he and I had as we began to develop the college library. Without Broughton's encouragement and help the first major revival of the

---

[320] Thomas A. Noble, *Tyndale House and Fellowship, the First Sixty Years* (Leicester: IVP, 2006). 43.

[321] Ibid., 44. quoting Douglas Johnson, a medical doctor who became the first General Secretary of the Inter-Varsity Fellowship in 1928. At the same meeting, Geoffrey Bromiley presented his proposal for 'study circles' in Old and New Testament and in Dogmatics, an idea which foreshadowed the eventual shape of what was to be the Tyndale Fellowship. His suggested list of established and younger scholars included Broughton Knox and Marcus Loane in the New Testament list and T C Hammond in the dogmatics list. Ibid p 45.

[322] The Rev Noel Pollard BA, BD (Syd), MA (Oxon), later the first Master of New College in the University of New South Wales.

[323] Broughton's widow.

library might never have happened. Each time I revisit
Moore the library is the most clear monument to his time
as Principal of the college and perhaps the most lasting.[324]

In 2016, the Moore College library collection numbers some 230,000
print volumes, 30,000 eBooks and subscriptions to more than 600
journals. This outstanding research collection will be in a new home by
the end of this year.

Faculty

When Broughton became principal, he was the only faculty member with
a doctorate. By the time he retired most of the faculty had PhDs from
prestigious overseas universities. Not only that, a number of his former
students held senior positions in other theological colleges so that David
Peterson could write to Ailsa:

> Broughton's influence continues throughout the world,
> with me in London, David[325] in Cape town, Peter[326] in
> Sydney and Graham[327] (Cole) in Melbourne, all following
> in his footsteps. He created a pattern for theological
> training that has not been matched anywhere else. We
> continue to thank God for him![328]

The College Committee

The corporate model of governance now common across the diocese was
not the template for conducting the business of managing the College for
most of the time Broughton was Principal. The Committee, clerical and

---

[324] Noel & Margaret Pollard letter to Ailsa Knox 15 January 1994 in the possession
of the writer.
[325] The Rev Dr David Seccombe, Principal, George Whitefield College 1993-2012.
[326] The Rev Dr Peter Jensen, Principal, Moore Theological College 1985-2001
later elected Archbishop of Sydney 2001-2013.
[327] The Rev Dr Graham Cole, Principal, Ridley College 1992-2001 and in 2016
Professor of Biblical and Systematic Theology at Trinity Evangelical Divinity
School USA.
[328] Letter (in the possession of the writer) from the Rev Dr David Peterson to
Ailsa Knox acknowledging congratulations on his appointment as Principal of
Oak Hill College. In this period, one should add the name of the Rev Dr Bruce
Winter, Warden, Tyndale House 1987-2006.

lay was elected by synod and three self-perpetuating trustees (being trustees of the Thomas Moore Estate) were additional members with a right to veto committee decisions. The principal was an ex officio member and the archbishop was always one of the trustees. It would be fair to say that Broughton viewed the Committee as a sounding board for advice rather than a policy making body.[329] My first serious encounter with Broughton and Moore College, was during the 1981 Synod when he asked if I be willing to have my name considered to fill a vacancy on the college Committee. Sometime after, the Diocesan Secretary informed me that I had been elected. I presented myself at 4.30 pm in the Cowper Room at the next meeting of the Committee. Archbishop Sir Marcus Loane was in the Chair. Completely without my knowledge, Broughton then moved that as the position of secretary was vacant due to the retirement of Peter Nicholson[330] 'that Robert Tong be invited to become the Secretary of the Committee.' I was duly stitched up.

Broughton and Marcus

During the period when Broughton's father, the Rev David Knox, was rector of St Paul's Chatswood (1924-1932), Marcus Loane, as a parishioner, would have become acquainted with the all the 'rectory children'. And as we know, in December 1937 he married Patricia the second eldest daughter. A close family acquaintance was now a brother-in-law. In February 1947 Broughton joined the College faculty as a junior lecturer. Of that time, Marcia Cameron observes

---

[329] After much negotiation, new ordinances were passed by the synod in 1985 which clarified the duties of the Moore College Board, the College Council having become a body corporate. While retaining the right to appoint the principal, the trustee's veto was surrendered. With further amendments to the governing ordinance and the winding up of the Thomas Moore Estate in 2010, the trustees ceased to exist.

[330] Peter Nicholson had been secretary for 25 years. He and Broughton were first cousins as his mother and Broughton's mother were sisters. Broughton's brother John married Sheila one of Peter's sisters. Another sister is Catherine Hamlin AC of Addis Ababa Fistula Hospital fame. The family tree can be explored by consulting the entry for Sir George Young in the 1985 edition of *Debrett's Peerage and Baronetage.* Sydney University conferred the degree of Doctor of Engineering *(honoris causa)* on Peter in 1993.

Marcus' many letters to Broughton make clear that they got on well. In his small, clear, meticulous writing he kept Broughton informed of College news and plans, asked for his advice and enjoyed discussing theological matters. As brothers-in-law they saw each other at family gatherings and their links were strengthened by Marcus' high regard for his mentor and former rector, David Knox. Broughton respected Marcus, who was his senior and his father's very capable former curate. Thus ties of marriage and friendship connected two of the College's four staff members.[331]

Broughton succeeded Marcus as Principal of Moore in 1959. Marcus was elected Archbishop of Sydney in 1966. A life-long friendship and family ties now had the overlay of Archbishop and Principal. While the responsibilities, duties and expectations of each office is different a close working relationship is essential for the life of the diocese. The Archbishop chairs the governing committee of the college, the Principal trains candidates for ordination, and both in their own office are theological leaders of the diocese.[332] Preservation of the evangelical character of the diocese was a given. I will leave it to others to comment on some theological differences such as 'fellowship' being the touchstone of Christian gatherings or the true understanding of 'ekklesia' in the New Testament. I will however, comment on another Maria Cameron passage relating to temporal matters under the remit of the college committee.

The friendship between Broughton and his brother-in-law Marcus Loane was severely tested, in a number of ways. One example is at the Moore College Committee meetings. As Archbishop of Sydney, Marcus Loane

---

[331] Cameron, *Enigmatic Life*, 96.
[332] As secretary of the college council since 1981, and a member of the Standing Committee of the synod of the diocese of Sydney since 1979, I have observed the working relationships between Principal Knox & Archbishop Loane, Principal Jensen & Archbishop Robinson, Principal Jensen & Archbishop Goodhew, Principal Woodhouse & Archbishop Jensen and Principal Thompson & Archbishop Davies. Each set of relationships was and is characterised by mutual trust, personal fellowship and an over-riding desire for the promulgation of the saving gospel of Jesus Christ.

presided, and it was clear that he was unhappy about the way bursary moneys were not awarded in the way they were intended. Loane was also opposed to the College's strategy of buying up property in Newtown and to something else that was happening in the 1970s - Broughton's encouragement of non-Anglican students to study at the College. Presbyterians in particular were entering the College for their theological training, and Loane feared that their influence would, in time, detract from the College's Anglican identity.[333]

Given the passage of some 30 years, I observe, on the three issues of contention, first, that the college council has a substantial sum soundly invested and accounted for, and with the yields appropriately allocated for scholarship assistance. Secondly, Broughton's territorial expansion delivered a significant property footprint. This has assisted in the funding of the magnificent new building next door. It also provides a measure of financial security for the future. Thirdly, training non-ordination students has provided a myriad of theologically equipped gospel workers for missionary service, student work, chaplaincies and the like.

Despite their official roles and areas of disagreement the foundation of deep friendship and family bonds was never under threat. The warmth of the relationship is evidenced by Marcus signing off a letter to Broughton 'I hope you continue to thrive. With affectionate greetings, Marcus.'[334]

Other Issues

Time precludes me from commenting on Broughton's impact on the Australian Anglican Church via the Doctrine Commission, the Canon Law Commission and the 'Red Book case' and not least the constitution for the Anglican Church of Australia. Closer to home there were the radio 2CH 'Protestant Faith' broadcasts and the founding of New College and

---

[333] Cameron, *Enigmatic Life*, 257. On this third issue, the Uniting Church of Australia was formed in 1977. The Methodists, Congregationalist and Presbyterians had small but viable colleges which were closed or amalgamated. The conservative element of the Presbyterian church declined to 'unite' and wanted to 'continue' so Moore provided the theological training for them.

[334] Letter (in the possession of the writer) from Patricia Loane to Broughton at Tyndale House where Marcus adds a postscript.

Robert Menzies College. Abroad, and almost single handed, the foundation of George Whitefield College Cape Town.

Broughton died on 14 January 1994. After a funeral service in St Andrew's Cathedral, where Marcus preached the sermon, he was laid to rest surrounded by family and friends. A hymn sung at the graveside had this refrain:

> Turn your eyes upon Jesus,
> Look full in His wonderful face,
> And the things of earth will grow strangely dim,
> In the light of His glory and grace.

That was a fitting summary of Broughton's ministry.

Bibliography

Armstrong, Brian G. *Calvinism and the Amyraut Heresy: Protestant Scholasticism and Humanism in Seventeenth-Century France.* Madison: University of Wisconsin Press, 1969.

Banks, Robert J. "The Theology of D.B. Knox—a Preliminary Estimate." In *God Who Is Rich in Mercy*, edited by Peter T. O'Brien and David G. Peterson. Hombush West, N.S.W.: Lancer Books, 1986.

Barth, Karl. *Church Dogmatics.* Edinburgh: T&T Clarke, 1974.

Baxter, Richard. *Aphorismes of Justification.* London, 1649.

Beasley-Murray, G.P. *Baptism in the New Testament.* London: Macmillan and Co, 1962.

Bediako, Kwame. *Jesus in Africa: The Christian Gospel in African History and Experience.* Cumbria: Paternoster, 2004.

Blacketer, Raymond A. "Blaming Beza: The Development of Definite Atonement in the Reformed Tradition." In *From Heaven He Came and Sought Her: Definite Atonement in Historical, Biblical, Theological, and Pastoral Perspective*, edited by David Gibson and Jonathan Gibson. 121-141. Wheaton: Crossway, 2013.

Boyer, Steven D. "Articulating Order: Trinitarian Discourse in an Egalitarian Age." *Pro Ecclesia* 18, no. 3 (2009): 255-256.

Bullinger, Heinrich. *In D. Apostoli Pauli Ad Thessalonicenses, Timotheum, Titum & Philemonem Epistolas.* Tiguri: Christ. Froschoverus, 1536.

———. *In D. Petri Apostoli Epistolam Utramque.* Tiguri: Froschoverum, 1534.

Calvin, John. *Commentaries on the Catholic Epistles.* Translated by John Owen. Edinburgh: Calvin Translation Society, 1855.

———. *Commentaries on the Epistles to Timothy, Titus, and Philemon.* Translated by William Pringle. Edinburgh: Calvin Translation Society, 1856.

———. *Institutes of the Christian Religion.* Translated by Ford Lewis Battles. edited by John T. McNeill Philadelphia: Westminster, 1960.

Cameron, Marcia. *An Enigmatic Life: David Broughton Knox: Father of Contemporary Sydney Anglicanism.* Brunswick East, Vic: Acorn Press, 2006.

Chambers, Neil A. "A Critical Examination of John Owen's Argument for

Limited Atonement in *the Death of Death in the Death of Christ.* " Unpublished M.Th., Reformed Theological Seminary, 1998.

Clifford, Alan C. *Atonement and Justification: English Evangelical Theology 1640-1790—an Evaluation.* Oxford: Oxford University Press, 1990.

Coffey, David. "The Holy Spirit as the Mutual Love of the Father and the Son." *Theological Studies* 51 (1990): 194-195.

Cole, Grahham. "The Doctrine of the Church: Towards Conceptual Clarification." In *Explorations 2: Church, Worship and the Local Congregation,* edited by B.G. Webb. Homebush, N.S.W.: Lancer, 1987.

Crisp, Oliver D. *Deviant Calvinism: Broadening Reformed Theology.* Minneapolis: Fortress Press, 2014.

Cunningham, William. *Works of William Cunningham.* Edinburgh: T&T Clark, 1863.

Dabney, R.L. *Syllabus and Notes of the Course of Systematic and Polemic Theology Taught in Union Theological Seminary, Virginia.* St. Louis: Presbyterian Publishing Company of St. Louis, 1878.

Davenant, John. "A Dissertation on the Death of Christ." Translated by Josiah Allport. In *An Exposition of the Epistle of St. Paul to the Colossians.* II.309-558. London: Hamilton, Adams and co., 1831.

Djaballah, Amar. "Controversy on Universal Grace: A Historical Survey of Moïse Amyraut's *Brief Traitté De La Predestination.*" 165-199, 2013.

Dumbrell, William J. *Covenant and Creation: An Old Testament Covenant Theology.* 2nd ed. Milton Keyynes: Paternoster, 2013.

———. "A Covenant with Creation (Genesis 6:18) and Jesus and the New Covenant (Luke 22:20)." *Reformed Theological Review* Supplement Series 2 (2007).

Dunn, James. "Once More Pistis Christou." In *Pauline Theology,* edited by E.E. Johnson and D.M. Hay. Atlanta: Scholars Press, 1997.

Foord, Martin. "God Wills All People to Be Saved - or Does He? Calvin's Reading of 1 Timothy 2:4." In *Engaging with Calvin: Aspects of the Reformer's Legacy for Today,* edited by Mark D. Thompson. 179-203. Leicester: Apollos, 2009.

Gatiss, Lee. "The Synod of Dort and Definite Atonement." In *From Heaven He Came and Sought Her: Definite Atonement in Historical, Biblical, Theological, and Pastoral Perspective,* edited by David Gibson and Jonathan Gibson. 143-163. Wheaton: Crossway, 2013.

Gentry, P.J., and S.J. Wellum. *God's Knigdom through God's Covenants*. Wheaton: Crossway, 2015.

Gibson, David, and Jonathan Gibson, eds. *From Heaven He Came and Sought Her: Definite Atonement in Historical, Biblical, Theological, and Pastoral Perspective*. Wheaton: Crossway, 2013.

Giles, Kevin. *What on Earth Is the Church?: An Exploration in New Testament Theology*. Eugene: Wipf & Stock, 1995.

Godfrey, W. Robert. "Tensions within International Calvinism: The Debate on the Atonement at the Synod of Dort, 1618-1619." Unpublished Ph.D., Stanford University, 1974.

Gomes, Alan W. "*De Jesu Christo Servatore*: Faustus Socinus on the Satisfaction of Christ." *Westminster Theological Journal* 55 (1993): 209-231.

Gunton, Colin E. *The Actuality of Atonement: A Study of Metaphor, Rationality and the Christian Tradition*. Edinburgh: T&T Clarke, 1988.

Hodge, Charles. *Systematic Theology*. New York: Charles Scribner and Company, 1872-3.

Jeffrey, Steve, Mike Ovey, and Andrew Sach. *Pierced for Our Transgressions: Rediscovering the Glory of Penal Substitution*. Nottingham: IVP, 2007.

Jensen, P. F. "Broughton Knox on Training for Ministry." In *D. Broughton Knox: Selected Works*, edited by Tony Payne. Sydney: Matthias Media, 2000.

———. "God and the Bible." In *The Enduring Authority of the Christian Scriptures*, edited by D. A. Carson. Grand Rapids: Eerdmans, 2016.

Knox, D. Broughton. "The Biblical Concept of Fellowship." In *Explorations 2: Church, Worship, and the Local Congregation*, edited by B.G. Webb. Sydney: Lancer, 1987.

———. "The Church, the Churches and the Denominations of the Churches." *Reformed Theological Review* 48 (1989): 15–25.

———. "De-Mythologizing the Church." *Reformed Theological Review* 32 (1973): 48–55.

———. *The Everlasting God*. Welwyn: Evangelical Press, 1982.

———. *Justification by Faith*. Sydney: Church Book Room, 1983 [1959].

———. *The Lord's Supper from Wycliffe to Cranmer*. Exeter: Paternoster, 1983.

———. *Selected Works*. edited by Tony Payne and Kirsten Birkett 2 vols Sydney: Matthias Media, 2000/2003.

———. *Sent by Jesus: Some Aspects of Christian Ministry Today.* Edinburgh: Banner of Truth, 1992.

———. *The Thirty-Nine Articles.* 2nd ed. Sydney: Anglican Information Office, 1976.

———. *The Thirty-Nine Articles: The Historic Basis of Anglican Faith.* 1st ed. London: Hodder and Stoughton, 1967.

Kuhn, Chase R. *The Ecclesiology of Donald Robinson and D. Broughton Knox: Exposition, Analysis and Theological Evaluation.* Eugene: Wipf & Stock, 2017.

Lawton, William. *The Better Time to Be: Utopian Attitudes to Society among Sydney Anglicans 1885-1914.* Kensington, NSW: UNSW Press, 1990.

———. "Nathaniel Jones." In *God Who Is Rich in Mercy: Essays Presented to Dr. D.B. Knox*, edited by Peter T. O'Brien and David G. Peterson. Hombush, N.S.W.: Lancer Books, 1986.

Leslie, Andrew M. "Christ's Faithfulness and Our Salvation." In *Donald Robinson Selected Works: Appreciation*, edited by Peter Bolt. Camperdown N.S.W.: Australian Church Record/Moore College, 2008.

Loane, Marcus. "Review of William Lawton's *Better Time to Be.*" *Lucas: An Evangelical History Review* no. 11 (Feb 1991).

———. *These Happy Warriors: Friends and Contemporaries.* Blackwood, S.A.: New Creations Publications, 1988.

Lynch, Michael. "Early Modern Hypothetical Universalism: Reflections on the *Status Quaestionis* and Modern Scholarship." In *Junius Institute Colloquium*. Calvin Theological Seminary, 2014.

Lynch, Michael J. "Not Satisfied: An Analysis and Response to Garry Williams on Penal Substitutionary Atonement and Definite Atonement." Grand Rapids: Calvin Theological Seminary, 2015.

Magezi, Chris. "The Conceptualization of Christ's Salvation in Kwame Bediako and Thomas F. Torrance and Its Implications for Spiritual Security in African Christianity" unpublished MA dissertation, North West University, 2015.

Milton, Anthony, ed. *The British Delegation and the Synod of Dort (1618-19).* Woodbridge: The Boydell Press, 2005.

Moo, Douglas J. *The Epistle to the Romans.* The New International Commentary on the New Testament. edited by Gordon Fee Grand Rapids: Eerdmans, 1996.

BIBLIOGRAPHY

———. *The Letters to the Colossians and to Philemon*. The Pillar New Testament Commentary. edited by D.A. Carson Grand Rapids: Eerdmans, 2008.

Moore, Jonathan D. *English Hypothetical Universalism: John Preston and the Softening of Reformed Theology.* Grand Rapids: Eerdmans, 2007.

———. "The Extent of the Atonement: English Hypothetical Universalism Versus Particular Redemption." In *Drawn into Controversie: Reformed Theological Diversity and Debates within Seventeenth-Century British Puritanism*, edited by Michael A.G. Haykin and Mark Jones. 124-161. Göttingen: Vandenhoeck & Ruprecht, 2011.

Morris, Leon. *Expository Reflections on the Letter to the Ephesians.* Grand Rapids: Baker Books, 1994.

Muller, Richard A. *Calvin and the Reformed Tradition: On the Work of Christ and the Order of Salvation.* Grand Rapids: Baker Academic, 2012.

Murray, John. "Covenant Theology." In *Collected Writings of John Murray: Volume Four.* 216-240. Edinburgh: Banner of Truth Trust, 1982.

Mwale, E. "A Theological Evaluation of T.F. Torrance's Understanding of the Humanity of Christ: The Free Divine Movement as a Paradigm for Understanding the Incarnational Vicarious Assumption of a Fallen Human Nature." unpublished MTh dissertation, North-West University, 2016.

Noble, Thomas A. *Tyndale House and Fellowship, the First Sixtyy Years.* Leicester: IVP, 2006.

O'Brien, Peter. *The Epistle to the Philippians: A Commentary on the Greek Text.* Grand Rapids: Eerdmans, 1991.

Owen, John. *The Works.* edited by William H. Goold Edinburgh: Johnstone & Hunter, 1850-1855.

Porter, Muriel. *Sydney Anglicans and the Threat to World Anglicanism.* Farnham, Surrey: Ashgate, 2011.

Snoddy, Richard. *The Soteriology of James Ussher: The Act and Object of Saving Faith.* Oxford: Oxford University Press, 2014.

Steele, David N., and Curtis C. Thomas. *The Five Points of Calvinism Defined, Defended and Documented.* Philadelphia: Presbyterian and Reformed, 1965.

Tay, Edwin E.M. *The Priesthood of Christ: Atonement in the Theology of John Owen (1616-1683).* Milton Keynes: Paternoster, 2014.

BIBLIOGRAPHY

Thompson, Mark D. "The Church of God and the Anglican Church of Australia." In *'Wonderfully and Confessedly Strange': Australian Essays in Anglican Ecclesiology*, edited by Bruce Kaye. Adelaide: ATF Press, 2006.

Torrance, T. F. *Incarnation: The Person and Life of Christ.* Milton Keynes: Paternoster, 2008.

Torrance, T.F. *The Trinitarian Faith.* Edinburgh: T&T Clark, 1993.

Trueman, Carl R. "Atonement and the Covenant of Redemption: John Owen on the Nature of Christ's Satisfaction." In *From Heaven He Came and Sought Her: Definite Atonement in Historical, Biblical, Theological, and Pastoral Perspective*, edited by David Gibson and Jonathan Gibson. 201-223. Wheaton: Crossway, 2013.

———. *The Claims of Truth: John Owen's Trinitarian Theology.* Carlisle: Paternoster, 1998.

———. *John Owen: Reformed Catholic, Renaissance Man.* Great Theologians Series. Aldershot: Ashgate, 2007.

Turretin, Francis. *Institutes of Elenctic Theology.* Translated by George Musgrave Giger. edited by James T. Dennison Jr. 3 vols Phillipsburg: P&R Publishing, 1992.

Tyndale, W. "The Obedience of a Christian Man." In *William Tyndale: Doctrinal Treatises*, edited by H. Walter. Cambridge: Parker Society, 1848.

Voetius, Gisbertus. *Selectarum Disputationum Theologicarum.* Five vols Utrecht: J. a Waesberge, 1648-67.

Wallace, Daniel B. *Greek Grammar: Beyond the Basics.* Grand Rapids: Zondervan, 1996.

Wenham, Gordon J. *Genesis 1-15.* Waco, TX: Word Books, 1987.

Williams, Garry J. "The Definite Intent of Penal Substitutionary Atonement." In *From Heaven He Came and Sought Her: Definite Atonement in Historical, Biblical, Theological, and Pastoral Perspective*, edited by David Gibson and Jonathan Gibson. 461-482. Wheaton: Crossway, 2013.

———. "The Punishment God Cannot Twice Inflict." In *From Heaven He Came and Sought Her: Definite Atonement in Historical, Biblical, Theological, and Pastoral Perspective*, edited by David Gibson and Jonathan Gibson. 483-515. Wheaton: Crossway, 2013.

Williams, S.K. "Again Πιστις Χριστου." *Catholic Biblical Quarterly* 49 (1987): 431-437.

Williams, Stephen. *The Election of Grace: A Riddle without a Resolution?* Grand Rapids: Eerdmans, 2015.

If you have enjoyed this book, you might like to consider:

- supporting the work of the Latimer Trust
- reading more of our publications
- recommending them to others

See www.latimertrust.org for more information.

Latimer Studies

LS 01	The Evangelical Anglican Identity Problem	Jim Packer
LS 02	The ASB Rite A Communion: A Way Forward	Roger Beckwith
LS 03	The Doctrine of Justification in the Church of England	Robin Leaver
LS 04	Justification Today: The Roman Catholic and Anglican Debate	R. G. England
LS 05/06	Homosexuals in the Christian Fellowship	David Atkinson
LS 07	Nationhood: A Christian Perspective	O. R. Johnston
LS 08	Evangelical Anglican Identity: Problems and Prospects	Tom Wright
LS 09	Confessing the Faith in the Church of England Today	Roger Beckwith
LS 10	A Kind of Noah's Ark? The Anglican Commitment to Comprehensiveness	Jim Packer
LS 11	Sickness and Healing in the Church	Donald Allister
LS 12	Rome and Reformation Today: How Luther Speaks to the New Situation	James Atkinson
LS 13	Music as Preaching: Bach, Passions and Music in Worship	Robin Leaver
LS 14	Jesus Through Other Eyes: Christology in a Multi-faith Context	Christopher Lamb
LS 15	Church and State Under God	James Atkinson,
LS 16	Language and Liturgy	Gerald Bray, Steve Wilcockson, Robin Leaver
LS 17	Christianity and Judaism: New Understanding, New Relationship	James Atkinson
LS 18	Sacraments and Ministry in Ecumenical Perspective	Gerald Bray
LS 19	The Functions of a National Church	Max Warren
LS19 (2nd ed.)	British Values and the National Church: Essays on Church and State from 1964-2014	Ed. David Holloway
LS 20/21	The Thirty-Nine Articles: Their Place and Use Today	Jim Packer, Roger Beckwith

LS 22	How We Got Our Prayer Book	T.W. Drury, Roger Beckwith
LS 23/24	Creation or Evolution: a False Antithesis?	Mike Poole, Gordon Wenham
LS 25	Christianity and the Craft	Gerard Moate
LS 26	ARCIC II and Justification	Alister McGrath
LS 27	The Challenge of the Housechurches	Tony Higton, Gilbert Kirby
LS 28	Communion for Children? The Current Debate	A. A. Langdon
LS 29/30	Theological Politics	Nigel Biggar
LS 31	Eucharistic Consecration in the First Four Centuries and its Implications for Liturgical Reform	Nigel Scotland
LS 32	A Christian Theological Language	Gerald Bray
LS 33	Mission in Unity: The Bible and Missionary Structures	Duncan McMann
LS 34	Stewards of Creation: Environmentalism in the Light of Biblical Teaching	Lawrence Osborn
LS 35/36	Mission and Evangelism in Recent Thinking: 1974-1986	Robert Bashford
LS 37	Future Patterns of Episcopacy: Reflections in Retirement	Stuart Blanch
LS 38	Christian Character: Jeremy Taylor and Christian Ethics Today	David Scott
LS 39	Islam: Towards a Christian Assessment	Hugh Goddard
LS 40	Liberal Catholicism: Charles Gore and the Question of Authority	G. F. Grimes
LS 41/42	The Christian Message in a Multi-faith Society	Colin Chapman
LS 43	The Way of Holiness 1: Principles	D. A. Ousley
LS 44/45	The Lambeth Articles	V. C. Miller
LS 46	The Way of Holiness 2: Issues	D. A. Ousley
LS 47	Building Multi-Racial Churches	John Root
LS 48	Episcopal Oversight: A Case for Reform	David Holloway
LS 49	Euthanasia: A Christian Evaluation	Henk Jochemsen
LS 50/51	The Rough Places Plain: AEA 1995	
LS 52	A Critique of Spirituality	John Pearce
LS 53/54	The Toronto Blessing	Martyn Percy

LS 55	The Theology of Rowan Williams	Garry Williams
LS 56/57	Reforming Forwards? The Process of Reception and the Consecration of Woman as Bishops	Peter Toon
LS 58	The Oath of Canonical Obedience	Gerald Bray
LS 59	The Parish System: The Same Yesterday, Today And For Ever?	Mark Burkill
LS 60	'I Absolve You': Private Confession and the Church of England	Andrew Atherstone
LS 61	The Water and the Wine: A Contribution to the Debate on Children and Holy Communion	Roger Beckwith, Andrew Daunton-Fear
LS 62	Must God Punish Sin?	Ben Cooper
LS 63	Too Big For Words? The Transcendence of God and Finite Human Speech	Mark D. Thompson
LS 64	A Step Too Far: An Evangelical Critique of Christian Mysticism	Marian Raikes
LS 65	The New Testament and Slavery: Approaches and Implications	Mark Meynell
LS 66	The Tragedy of 1662: The Ejection and Persecution of the Puritans	Lee Gatiss
LS 67	Heresy, Schism & Apostasy	Gerald Bray
LS 68	Paul in 3D: Preaching Paul as Pastor, Story-teller and Sage	Ben Cooper
LS69	Christianity and the Tolerance of Liberalism: J.Gresham Machen and the Presbyterian Controversy of 1922-1937	Lee Gatiss
LS70	An Anglican Evangelical Identity Crisis: The Churchman–Anvil Affair of 1981-4	Andrew Atherstone
LS71	Empty and Evil: The worship of other faiths in 1 Corinthians 8-10 and today	Rohintan Mody
LS72	To Plough or to Preach: Mission Strategies in New Zealand during the 1820s	Malcolm Falloon
LS73	Plastic People: How Queer Theory is changing us	Peter Sanlon
LS74	Deification and Union with Christ: Salvation in Orthodox and Reformed thought	Slavko Eždenci
LS75	As It Is Written: Interpreting the Bible with Boldness	Benjamin Sargent
LS76	Light From Dark Ages? An Evangelical Critique of Celtic Spirituality	Marian Raikes
LS77	The Ethics of Usury	Ben Cooper

LS78	For Us and For Our Salvation: 'Limited Atonement' in the Bible, Doctrine, History and Ministry	Lee Gatiss
LS79	Positive Complementarianism: The Key Biblical Texts	Ben Cooper
LS80	Were they Preaching 'Another Gospel'? Justification by faith in the Second Century	Andrew Daunton-Fear
LS81	Thinking Aloud: Responding to the Contemporary Debate about Marriage, Sexuality and Reconciliation	Martin Davie
LS82	Spells, Sorcerers and Spirits: Magic and the Occult in the Bible	Kirsten Birkett
LS83	Your Will Be Done: Exploring Eternal Subordination, Divine Monarchy and Divine Humility	M.J Ovey
LS84	Resilience: A Spiritual Project	Kirsten Birkett

Latimer Briefings

LB01	The Church of England: What it is, and what it stands for	R. T. Beckwith
LB02	Praying with Understanding: Explanations of Words and Passages in the Book of Common Prayer	R. T. Beckwith
LB03	The Failure of the Church of England? The Church, the Nation and the Anglican Communion	A. Pollard
LB04	Towards a Heritage Renewed	H.R.M. Craig
LB05	Christ's Gospel to the Nations: The Heart & Mind of Evangelicalism Past, Present & Future	Peter Jensen
LB06	Passion for the Gospel: Hugh Latimer (1485–1555) Then and Now. A commemorative lecture to mark the 450th anniversary of his martyrdom in Oxford	A. McGrath
LB07	Truth and Unity in Christian Fellowship	Michael Nazir-Ali
LB08	Unworthy Ministers: Donatism and Discipline Today	Mark Burkill
LB09	Witnessing to Western Muslims: A Worldview Approach to Sharing Faith	Richard Shumack
LB10	Scarf or Stole at Ordination? A Plea for the Evangelical Conscience	Andrew Atherstone
LB11	How to Write a Theology Essay	Michael P. Jensen

LB12	Preaching: A Guidebook for Beginners	Allan Chapple
LB13	Justification by Faith: Orientating the Church's teaching and practice to Christ (Toon Lecture 1)	Michael Nazir-Ali
LB14	"Remember Your Leaders": Principles and Priorities for Leaders from Hebrews 13	Wallace Benn
LB15	How the Anglican Communion came to be and where it is going	Michael Nazir-Ali
LB16	Divine Allurement: Cranmer's Comfortable Words	Ashley Null
LB17	True Devotion: In Search of Authentic Spirituality	Allan Chapple
LB18	Commemorating War and Praying for Peace: A Christian reflection on the Armed Forces	John Neal
LB19	A Better Vision: Resources for the debate about human sexuality in the Church of England	Ed. Martin Davie
LB20	Transgender Liturgies: Should the Church of England develop liturgical materials to mark gender transition?	Martin Davie
LB22	Ministry Under the Microscope: The What, Why, and How of Christian Ministry	Allan Chapple

Anglican Foundations Series

FWC	The Faith We Confess: An Exposition of the 39 Articles	Gerald Bray
AF02	The 'Very Pure Word of God': The Book of Common Prayer as a Model of Biblical Liturgy	Peter Adam
AF03	Dearly Beloved: Building God's People Through Morning and Evening Prayer	Mark Burkill
AF04	*Day by Day: The Rhythm of the Bible in the Book of Common Prayer*	Benjamin Sargent
AF05	The Supper: Cranmer and Communion	Nigel Scotland
AF06	A Fruitful Exhortation: A Guide to the Homilies	Gerald Bray
AF07	*Instruction in the Way of the Lord: A Guide to the Prayer Book Catechism*	Martin Davie
AF08	Till Death Us Do Part: "The Solemnization of Matrimony" in the Book of Common Prayer	Simon Vibert
AF09	'Sure and Certain Hope': Death and Burial in the Book of Common Prayer	Andrew Cinnamond

Latimer Books

GGC	God, Gays and the Church: Human Sexuality and Experience in Christian Thinking	eds. Lisa Nolland, Chris Sugden, Sarah Finch
WTL	The Way, the Truth and the Life: Theological Resources for a Pilgrimage to a Global Anglican Future	eds. Vinay Samuel, Chris Sugden, Sarah Finch
AEID	Anglican Evangelical Identity – Yesterday and Today	J.I.Packer, N.T.Wright
IB	The Anglican Evangelical Doctrine of Infant Baptism	John Stott, Alec Motyer
BF	Being Faithful: The Shape of Historic Anglicanism Today	Theological Resource Group of GAFCON
TPG	The True Profession of the Gospel: Augustus Toplady and Reclaiming our Reformed Foundations	Lee Gatiss
SG	Shadow Gospel: Rowan Williams and the Anglican Communion Crisis	Charles Raven
TTB	Translating the Bible: From William Tyndale to King James	Gerald Bray
PWS	Pilgrims, Warriors, and Servants: Puritan Wisdom for Today's Church	ed. Lee Gatiss
PPA	Preachers, Pastors, and Ambassadors: Puritan Wisdom for Today's Church	ed. Lee Gatiss
CWP	The Church, Women Bishops and Provision: The Integrity of Orthodox Objections to the Proposed Legislation Allowing Women Bishops	
TSF	The Truth Shall Set You Free: Global Anglicans in the 21st Century	ed. Charles Raven
LMM	*Launching Marsden's Mission: The Beginnings of the Church Missionary Society in New Zealand, viewed from New South Wales*	eds. Peter G Bolt David B. Pettett
MST1	*Listen To Him: Reading and Preaching Emmanuel in Matthew*	Ed. Peter Bolt
GWC	*The Genius of George Whitefield: Reflections on his Ministry from 21st Century Africa*	Ed. Benjamin Dean & Adriaan Neele

172

Lightning Source UK Ltd.
Milton Keynes UK
UKHW01f0657250818
327806UK00002B/98/P